THE OLD LODGES & HOTELS OF OUR NATIONAL PARKS

THE OLD LODGES & HOTELS OF OUR NATIONAL PARKS

Bill McMillon

ICARUS PRESS
South Bend, Indiana
1983

THE OLD LODGES & HOTELS OF OUR NATIONAL PARKS

Manufactured in the United States of America

Unless otherwise stated, all photos are by Bill McMillon.

Icarus Press, Inc.
Post Office Box 1225
South Bend, Indiana 46624

1 2 3 4 5 6 7 87 86 85 84 83

Library of Congress Cataloging in Publication Data

McMillon, Bill 1942-
The old hotels and lodges of our national parks.

Includes index.
1. Hotels, taverns, etc.—United States. 2. National
parks and reserves—United States. I. Title.
TX909.M34 1983 647'.947301 83-18456
ISBN 0-89651-551-6

To Mary—
for coming up with the idea;
and Matt—
for putting up with the travel.

Contents

Preface

I HAVE ONE REGRET LEFT FROM THE HUNDREDS OF MILES I TRAVELED throughout the country while doing research for this book—I was not conscientious enough in noting all the names of the many National Park Service and private concessionaire employees who went out of their way to help me glean useful information about the lodges and hotels. They were my primary source of information, and all who helped deserve to be mentioned by name. Unfortunately I don't remember them all, so, rather than leave some out, I am just going to say a combined thank you to all who helped me as I wandered around the parks trying to piece a history of the old lodges and hotels.

So little has been written about these lodges that people had to be my primary resource, and I am thankful for that. Otherwise I would never have met the many employees of both the NPS and the concessionaires who were glad that someone was finally recording some of the history of the lodges. They knew that few visitors ever discovered the many tidbits about the early histories of the lodges that give the lodges their special ambiences, and they wanted guests to feel that ambience as they, who spend their work hours in the lodges, felt it.

Bill McMillon

Introduction

SEVERAL YEARS AGO MY FAMILY AND I TOOK A CAMPING TRIP THROUGH Oregon. On the trip we decided to visit the Oregon Caves National Monument, and as much as we liked the caves, we were more impressed by the Oregon Caves Chateau located at the monument. The chateau is an old lodge. Built years ago to house the hardy tourists who made the long and arduous trek to see the caves, it still serves today as a stopover for tourists visiting there, and it retains its original rustic charm—complete with courtyard trout pond and peeled-pine poles in the interior.

A few days after having lunch at the Oregon Caves Chateau we were sitting in the lounge of the Crater Lake Lodge. It was undergoing an extensive renovation to bring it up to present-day safety standards, as has taken place over the past decade with many of our national park lodges constructed early in the century.

While looking out over Crater Lake, my wife mentioned that a book about the old lodges of the national parks would make a good gift for relatives in the Midwest, and would even be helpful to us. We hadn't even known that the Oregon Caves Chateau existed.

We couldn't find such a book on our trip, nor after we returned home. Further research showed that no book covering all the old lodges and hotels of the parks had ever been written.

What a loss, we felt. By then we knew that there were about two dozen of the old lodges still in operation, and we knew that at least several of them had aged gracefully over the past half-century. It was then I decided to write my own book.

I wanted a book that reflected the gentility of these old lodges, that portrayed them as part of a less-hectic era when travelers braved long, often hazardous journeys to view the wonders of our fledgling national park system. They wanted comfortable lodgings after they reached their destinations. However, as the lodges and hotels from that period show, what was considered comfortable in the early 1900s was obviously different from what many of us consider comfortable today.

Many of today's tourists make one-day sweeps through the parks, spending their nights in the plastic-and-chrome comfort (if you can call it comfort) of Holiday Inns and Howard Johnson Motels. Tourists of the late 1800s and early 1900s didn't have that luxury. Travel was slow, and distances to the parks were long. While a large number of early visitors, moving through the parks on "Grand Tours," stayed only a short while at any one lodge, others stayed for weeks—or even months—at one lodge. Accordingly, the lodges and hotels of that period were built with an opulence that offered comforts to satisfy the most fastidious guests.

Today some of the rooms seem small and poorly equipped, but the lodges still offer large sitting rooms, verandas, mezzanines, and good restaurants you just don't find at modern motels.

It wasn't always possible for the "common tourist" to enjoy the luxury of some of these lodges. When The Ahwahnee opened in 1927 there was an English butler on the staff by the name of Clark, whose duty it was to treat all nonguests with the condescension that could only come from an English butler. Part of his job was to see that the great unwashed weren't even allowed in the lobby of the hotel, where they might offend the paying guests.

Today any of us can visit, stay at, or eat our meals at all the lodges and hotels in our national parks. Some are still out of the common tourist's price range, but others are even less expensive than the plastic-and-chrome lodgings on the fringes of the parks.

You don't have to spend the night at these lodges to get a feel of the charm they exude or the leisure that early guests enjoyed. An afternoon drink or a late dinner in a dining room built for slow, leisurely meals—rather than fast service—can give you an idea of what these lodges must have been like half a century ago.

[3] Early History of the Lodges and Hotels

MOST OF THE LODGES AND HOTELS COVERED IN THIS BOOK WOULDN'T BE built in our national parks today. The concepts that govern construction of lodging in the parks have changed greatly in the past half century, and even the idea of constructing a fancy hotel on the rim of the Grand Canyon or close to a natural attraction such as Old Faithful would bring howls of protests from conservationist groups. And rightly so. Our natural wonders are too precious to destroy by erecting huge buildings near them.

Although I am in agreement with the move toward less commercialism in our parks, I wouldn't want to see any of the old lodges that remain, from the dozens that were built in the early years of the park system, torn down because of the change in park policy. They are now part of the heritage of our parks, and should be viewed as such.

Today all of the lodges in this book are under the jurisdiction of park administrators, and the concessionaires who either lease or own the buildings must abide by stringent regulations concerning the way the lodges are operated. This hasn't always been the case. The construction and operation of some of the lodges in this book were as noted for the abuse of park service rules as for the observation of them. Other lodges were built before the surrounding land was designated as a park, and were slowly assimilated into the park service.

All of the lodges, however, were built so that tourists of the late 1800s and early 1900s could enjoy a restful visit to one of our national wonders, and the National Park Service has slowly—and sometimes reluctantly—taken over the supervision of their operations in the past fifty years. The lodges have been operated by a number of concessionaires over the years, and most have maintained the lodges with care. Some, though, neglected theirs, and the NPS has had to replace them with new concessionaires who have attempted to renovate the lodges so they approach the standards that guests expect of such traditions.

There were many more lodges in the parks in earlier years, but these disappeared because of disaster and neglect. Others became outdated in the eyes of the NPS and concessionaires in the fifties and sixties and were torn down, to be replaced by more modern facilities.

The twenty-two lodges and hotels in this book are the only remaining ones that retain enough of their original structures to be considered representative of the early years of the national parks. Others, such as Zion Canyon Lodge, Rock Harbor Lodge at Isle Royal, and Mammoth Cave Hotel, still have part of their original structure, but so much has been replaced that the ambience of the earlier period has been lost.

Still others, such as Mt. McKinley Lodge and the Grand Canyon Hotel in Yellowstone, have been destroyed by fire and earthquake in the past thirty years.

The decades of the forties, fifties, and sixties were a period of deterioration and neglect for the old lodges as tourists forsook the old and patronized the new. Both concessionaires and the NPS lost interest in preserving the old lodges as the NPS moved into a period where buildings in the parks became much less important than in previous decades.

Americans rediscovered their past in the seventies, and the old lodges and hotels in the national parks made a comeback as tourists decided that it was more fun to spend a night in a room without a bath but filled with a sense of history than to spend the night in a Holiday Inn.

This resurgence of interest in the lodges forced the NPS and the concessionaires to reevaluate their fiscal priorities and to set aside large sums of money to renovate the lodges—not only to make them safe, but to restore a number of them to their original state.

The restored and renovated lodges and hotels presented in this book, each within the fuller context of the parks or monuments in which they are to be found, recreate in large measure that lost gentility of the early years of our national parks. The lodges were all built at least fifty years ago, have not been remodeled to the extent that their original charm was erased, and are operated by concessionaires under the supervision of the National Park Service. To the traveler of today, they afford a stirring glimpse of a grand yet rusticated life that was.

Photos of the lodges accompany the text, and reservation information for each, together with some commentary, is given in the appendix.

[5]

Crater Lake National Park

IN 1980 MT. ST. HELENS REMINDED US THAT VOLCANOES CAN BLOW THEIR tops, and that they unleash massive amounts of energy when they do—energy that destroys all within reach of the eruption. Crater Lake is a result of just such an eruption—one many times more powerful than the Mt. St. Helens' eruption—that occurred about 12,000 years ago. Soon after the violent eruption the top of the volcano collapsed to form a large caldera.

This caldera filled with water after subsequent small eruptions sealed off the vents in the center of the crater. Rain and snowmelt have since combined to fill the crater with almost 2,000 feet of clear blue water. The lake, the deepest in the United States, and surrounding land, was designated as a national park in 1902, and within a decade a large lodge was built on the south rim of the crater to house the increasing number of tourists who visited the new park.

CRATER LAKE LODGE

Most tourists who visit Crater Lake drive in, look over the rim of the caldera, comment on how blue the lake is, and drive away, hardly staying long enough to get a feel for the flora and fauna of the park surrounding the lake. They don't know what they are missing; not only the many miles of trails in the park that carry you into the back country, but the more restful activities of the park. Activities like watching a full moon rise over the eastern rim of the caldera to reflect on the dark waters of the lake far below, or watching a sunrise from one of the lakeside rooms of the Crater Lake Lodge.

These are simple pleasures, but pleasures that tourists in the early 1900s found after they spent long hours traveling on poor roads from Medford and Grant's Pass to reach Crater Lake.

Until 1915 those tourists had to settle for tents and tent cabins during their stay at the lake, but the NPS and several local investors realized the need for more comfortable lodging for tourists who were willing to pay. And that was what Crater Lake Lodge was designed to be.

Little is known of the early plans of the lodge, but it is known
that construction began on it in 1911. Because of the long hard **[6]**
winters at Crater Lake—there is often a heavy snowpack well into July—and because of poor access roads to the lake, construction went slowly on the massive stone-and-shingle building. It was a full four years after construction began before the lodge was opened to guests.

The building was typical of the lodges built in the national parks in the early 1900s. The rooms weren't spacious—in fact, they would even be considered small by today's standards—but the lobby was huge and warmed by what is said to be the largest

The rear of the lodge sits right on the edge of the caldera rim.

From the front, the lodge appears to be just another hotel, with little indication of the view from the rear (left). The walls in the lobby and stairway to the upper floors are made of unbarked fir slabs (right).

fireplace in Oregon, and the dining room was cheerful.

The unbarked logs that lined the stairways and lobby added a warmth to the lobby that was needed during the chilly mornings and evenings, and they gave the lodge the rustic feeling that all the lodges in the parks of the period attempted to present.

Most of the rooms lacked modern conveniences such as bathrooms, but that didn't bother the guests of the day. They didn't expect such conveniences, and were very satisfied with what the lakeside rooms offered—a view of the deep blue waters of Crater Lake.

So many guests came to the lodge that the west wing was added in 1923 to accomodate them.

Little has changed at the lodge since that addition was completed, although more rooms have had baths added. Also, the NPS has recently spent over $300,000 to bring the lodge up to code for fire and safety standards. Unfortunately, one aspect of that upgrading was that the fireplace in the lobby was declared unsafe and guests no longer have the pleasure of sitting in front of its blazing flames on a cool evening.

Until the late forties the lodge offered nightly entertainment for its guests, but today this is limited to an occasional ranger talk in the large lobby. Guests are expected to furnish their own entertainment, and since most of the lodge's guests spend only a night, or at the most two, there is little demand for the type of entertainment that guests who spent several weeks at the lodge [8]
expected.

The renovations on the lodge added fire escapes to the outside of the building, but other than that the lodge appears as it did when it was completed in 1923. The large native stones and cedar shingles blend with the volcanic rock along the rim of the crater, and nothing has been changed between the lodge and the rim. Primarily because there isn't any room. The lodge sits right on the edge of the rim, and it offers an unimpeded view of the blue waters of Crater Lake and the steep sides of the crater that jut thousands of feet above the water.

[9] Death Valley National Monument

EVERYONE'S HEARD OF DEATH VALLEY—AN AREA OF UNBEARABLE HEAT IN the summer and where two inches of rain means that the raindrops fell two inches apart on the ground. The area is known for its inhospitality, not its hospitality, and it seems an unlikely spot for a resort hotel.

It is indeed hot in the summer—it holds the record for the highest temperature ever recorded in the U.S., 134°F in July 1913; and it is dry—there have been years with *no* measurable precipitation. This doesn't mean that no tourists ever visit there, however.

Some days of the year—three-day winter weekends, Thanksgiving weekend, and the weeks of Christmas and New Year's—over 10,000 people descend upon the camping facilities in the valley. Easter Week, particularly in a wet year, is even busier, for tourists not only to enjoy the balmy desert weather, they also hope to see a profusion of desert wildflowers.

Few of these thousands of tourists stay in hotels, for there are only three in Death Valley. Most camp or park their recreational vehicles in designated campgrounds in the monument. Others make single-day visits to the valley on their way to other destinations.

Some do stay in hotels, though, and one of those, the Furnace Creek Inn, ranks among the most luxurious inns in the national park system.

FURNACE CREEK INN

Furnace Creek wasn't built under the auspices of the National Park Service. Even in 1927 the NPS would have been reluctant to

The Furnace Creek Inn overlooks a broad expanse of Death Valley.

build a full-fledged resort hotel in a monument or park (although The Ahwahnee had just opened in Yosemite), and that is what Furnace Creek Inn was, and is. It has a spring-fed swimming pool that is a constant 90°F, several tennis courts, an eighteen-hole golf course, and most of the other amenities offered by desert resorts in Palm Springs and Scottsdale.

The resorts in Palm Springs and Scottsdale were built close to major transportation arteries so that guests would have easy access to them. Furnace Creek Inn was built in a wilderness. A wilderness little removed from the dangers of death from heat and thirst recorded in the stories of early travelers in the region. Those stories had continued to fascinate most Americans well into the 1900s, and there was great awe and respect for the hardy miners who worked the borax mines in the valley until the mid-1920s.

There was also a great curiosity about how those miners were able to survive the extremes of Death Valley, and more and more tourists began to visit the area as railroads and automobiles made the American public more mobile. These tourists ventured into Death Valley to experience the wilderness of the area and the possible dangers that lurked there. Not that most really wanted danger, just the possibility of it was enough to satisfy their needs.

There were no facilities in the region to house the increasing

[11]

Comfortable furniture and large windows make the lobby of the inn a pleasant place to view the valley.

number of tourists who were making the effort to visit the valley, and officials of the Pacific Coast Borax Company, who owned and operated the borax mines in the valley, realized the potential profits that could be made from a luxury hotel for the more affluent tourists.

They decided to explore the possibility of building such a facility, and since they had no experience with hotels they hired Nellie Coffman of the world-famous Desert Inn of Palm Springs as a consultant. She was a recognized authority on desert resorts, and she supervised architect Albert Martin as he drew up plans for the Furnace Creek Inn.

The board of directors for Pacific Coast Borax was reluctant to give final approval for construction of the inn, for the $30,000 price tag was considered too high. But under pressure from Coffman, who thought that the inn would make an excellent resort, the board did give final approval for the project in 1925.

Work began soon afterward as a group of Panamint Indians, residents of Death Valley with plenty of experience in construction in the area, started making the thousands of adobe bricks to be used in the building of the Furnace Creek Inn. While these bricks were still being formed and before construction of the inn was half completed, the first manager and crew of the inn were hired.

An official of Pacific Coast Borax, Frank Jenifer, had visited Horace Albright, future director of the National Park Service and then superintendent of Yellowstone National Park, and mentioned the company's plans for their new luxury hotel. Jenifer told Albright that the company was having difficulty finding a manager with the right experience to run the Furnace Creek Inn for them.

Albright suggested he might have just the person for the job. In [12]
fact, he thought he might have a complete trained crew to go with the manager. Old Faithful Lodge in Yellowstone was open only during the summer months, and the Furnace Creek Inn was going to be open only during the winter months. Albright suggested that Jenifer talk to Beulah Brown, manager of Old Faithful Lodge, and her crew about working both places.

Since the seasons of the two didn't overlap, Ms. Brown and her entire crew were willing to work at the Furnace Creek Inn. Jenifer hired them on the spot, even though the inn wasn't completed.

Work progressed quickly on the construction, however, after

The light fixture and mirror frame are both examples of handcrafted features of the Inn.

the adobe bricks were formed, and most of the building was completed by January 1927. The inn fit in well with the austere landscape of Death Valley. The adobe bricks of the walls merged with the soil of the hillsides from which the clay had been dug to make them, the red-tiled roof added another desert hue to the building, and the large stone walls around the facility were built of native stone.

The architect had designed a resort that met all the requirements of the affluent tourists who would soon flock to the Fur-
[13] nace Creek Inn. The inn fit the mood of the desert and would soon offer opulence and service to match any hotel in the United States or Europe. Soon, but not when it opened its doors to guests in February 1927. Many of the fine furnishings for the spacious rooms had yet to arrive when the first guests registered, and workers were still busy completing the building.

Among those workers was stonemason Steve Esteves, a native of Death Valley around whom some mystery has since grown. He continued to do masonry work around the inn for many years, and he was buried nearby upon his death.

Employees of both Fred Harvey Company and the NPS know of Esteves and will tell how to find his grave, but they all refuse to divulge anything about his life. His works stand for all to see, particularly the large stone walls he built, but Fred Harvey employees refer people to the NPS when they make queries about Esteves, and the NPS employees refer them on to Pauline Esteves, the stonemason's daughter, who still lives in the Death Valley area.

No one seems to know why all these referrals are made, but there is an undercurrent of mystery that is buried in secrecy. Whatever the real story behind Esteve's life, and the secrecy that surrounds it, he has left his legacy in the many stone walls both inside and outside the Furnace Creek Inn.

By the 1928 season Esteves and the other workers had completed their work on the original buildings of the Furnace Creek Inn, and Beulah Brown had her crew dressed in starched black uniforms and trained them to serve the most demanding guests. Along with the furnishings that now filled the interior of the inn, the staff truly made Furnace Creek Inn the match of any luxury hotel in the United States or Europe.

Pacific Coast Borax advertised the Furnace Creek Inn heavily in those pre-Depression days, and tourists began to fill it quickly. Most of these guests were people who had been intrigued with the tales of Death Valley and the spirit of adventure surrounding

The stark mountains of the valley are visible from many locations at the inn. This scene is from the lounge.

those tales. After staying at Furnace Creek Inn in the isolation of Death Valley, many were more than intrigued—they were captivated. Captivated by its setting and its opulence.

Many of these returned to the inn for many other visits over the years, and this is still true. Over 80 percent of the guests at the inn today are repeat guests. There are even three couples who have returned to the inn on the same date to say in the same room for the past thirty-seven years. Not all of the returnees are that dedicated, but the Furnace Creek Inn does have the highest return rate of any of the lodges featured in this book. Only The Ahwahnee approaches it.

The magnetism of Death Valley and the Furnace Creek Inn is

as strong today as ever. During the busy weeks of the winter season it is almost impossible to get reservations sooner than a full year before the date you wish to stay at the inn. Guests obviously enjoy the spaciousness of the rooms, the genteel service of the staff, and the comfort of the adobe structure.

The interior of the inn is whitewashed stucco with tile floors and open-beam ceilings. The lobby has an imposing fireplace near the registration desk, and its front windows offer a view of the broad expanse of Death Valley.

[15] Both the dining room and lounge retain the quiet dignity that the inn has become famous for, and guests must dress for dinner. For men this means jackets, and for women, no Levis.

While today's guests almost all arrive at the inn by automobile, this wasn't always the case. When the inn opened in 1927 the roads into death Valley were poor, and often treacherous. Pacific Coast Borax owned several small railroads used to transport borax from their mines to their processing plants. They decided to promote these as the best means of reaching Furnace Creek Inn.

It wasn't unusual for resorts of the day to somehow be involved with railroads. In fact, railroads were very involved in the construction of several of the lodges in this book (see chapters on Glacier National Park, Grand Canyon National Park, and Yellowstone National Park). Pacific Coast Borax was unusual only in that they were converting what was previously an all-freight railroad to one that also carried a number of passengers.

Pacific Coast Borax had to have some way to get passengers to their short lines, however, so they worked out a deal with two transcontinental railroads, the Union Pacific and the Santa Fe, to have them promote tours to the Furnace Creek Inn. The UP and Santa Fe promoted the tours and carried the passengers to the junction of their lines with the Tonopah and Tidewater Railroad, one of Pacific Coast Borax's railroads. The passengers then transferred to the Tonopah and Tidewater, which carried them to Death Valley Junction on the west side of the valley. From there they rode gas-powered railcars to what is now the ghost town of Ryan. They finished their trip to the Furnace Creek Inn in open touring cars.

This was a long and complicated trip, but most who made it were more than pleased. The accommodations and service at the inn were superb, its setting was unmatched anywhere in the country because of its isolation, and it offered jaded tourists an experience that was unbelievable—a majestic resort in desolate, and sometimes dangerous, country.

As more and more tourists visited Death Valley and the Furnace Creek Inn, and as Pacific Coast Borax moved many of its mining operations out of the area, a move to declare the valley a national monument gained strength.

Death Valley was designated a national monument in 1933 by Franklin Roosevelt, seven years after the Furnace Creek Inn opened its doors to guests.

Today, over fifty years after its opening, the inn is still offering guests the same first-class service it offered when Beulah Brown's
crew opened the inn. The difference is that Death Valley is now a **[16]**
national monument, and the Furnace Creek Inn is owned and operated by the Fred Harvey Company.

Not much else has changed. The spring-fed fish pond in the garden is still an inviting place to linger on a warm evening, and the rest of the amenities of a first-class resort are still offered by the inn.

Furnace Creek is the only lodge within the jurisdiction of the NPS that can truly be classified as a first-class resort. This doesn't mean that anyone is excluded. It's just that all guests have to pay for the opulence and service of the inn—over $150 per day per person. Of course that is on the American Plan, where breakfast and dinner are offered.

If you don't want to spend that kind of money you can visit the inn, sit in the lobby where you can gaze upon a panorama of Death Valley, have a drink in the lounge which has stone walls that were built by Steve Esteves, or eat in the semi-formal dining room—with reservations, of course.

Either way, enjoy, for Furnace Creek Inn is one of a kind, the only truly exclusive resort in our national parks.

[17]

Glacier National Park

RAILROADS WERE INVOLVED WITH THE CONSTRUCTION OF HOTELS AND lodges in our national parks from the time the first park, Yellowstone, was designated in 1872, but nowhere more than at Glacier National Park. If it hadn't been for Louis W. Hill, president of the Great Northern Railway in the early 1900s, there would not be the famous lodges of Glacier. In fact, there might not even be a Glacier National Park.

Hill had several reasons for being involved with the Glacier area. As a conservationist he wanted to preserve the vast wilderness area of northwest Montana for future generations, and as president of the Great Northern he wanted to increase passenger traffic on his railroad.

These two interests provided Hill with plenty of reasons to push for the development of Glacier as a national park, but there were many people in Montana who suspected there was only one really important reason to Hill—economic gain. Louis' father, James J. Hill, had preceded him as president of the railroad and had been involved in extensive subterfuge regarding the acquisition of various properties for the Great Northern. The people of Montana felt that Louis was little different from his father and feared that he was so interested in making money that he would do so at the expense of the park.

But Louis was different from his father and was honest about his intentions. While James seemed unable to do anything above board if it could be done on the sly, Louis was open and spoke to a conference on national parks, held at Yellowstone in 1911, about his interests in the parks. At that conference he said, "The railroads are greatly interested in the passenger traffic to the parks. Every passenger that goes to the national parks, wherever he may be, represents practically a net earning."

Since railroads were about the only way most tourists could reach the parks, this meant that any expansion of park facilities only increased railway profits. And Louis Hill, no less than any railway magnate, wanted to increase his profits.

He saw a chance to do that at Glacier and began a campaign to get the right to build lodges in the park as soon as it was designated. Since he had been a powerful force in the effort to get Glacier declared a park, and since he had strong political influence in the Northwest, Hill had little trouble gaining that right.

Hill invested much time, and more money, in building a series of chalets and lodges along the east side of Glacier National Park in the first six years after it was designated a park. Between 1911 and 1917 he constructed several small chalet-type lodges, and two large lodges. These lodges were Glacier Park Lodge, built at Midvale (now East Glacier), and Many Glacier Hotel, constructed on the shore of Swiftcurrent Lake.

These were the two largest lodges built in Glacier by the Great Northern, and the only two of the original lodges constructed by Hill in the first decade of the park that are still standing.

Hill wanted to build one other hotel on the east side of the Continental Divide, but it was outside his normal sphere of influence. In fact, it wasn't even in the United States, but across the U.S. border in Canada.

Scenic wonders often cross national boundaries, and that is certainly true where the northern boundary of Glacier National Park is also the international boundary between the United States and Canada. When Glacier was designated a national park in 1910 its northern boundary coincided with the southern boundary of a "forest park" that had been designated by the Canadian government in 1895, the Waterton Lakes National Park.

Hill, as others both before and after him, felt that the two parks were simply an extension of one another, and wanted to build another major hotel at Waterton Lakes to compliment his holdings in Glacier National Park. The Canadian government was reluctant to give Hill, and a U.S. railroad, the right to build a hotel in a Canadian park, and it wasn't until the mid-1920s that Hill got the go-ahead from the Canadians to begin construction on a new hotel at Waterton.

That hotel was to be the Prince-of-Wales Hotel, completed in 1927. Many Canadians are surprised to learn today that it was a U.S. railroad rather than a Canadian one that built the hotel.

With the completion of the Prince-of-Wales, Hill had built his last major hotel in the Glacier area, but the Glacier Park Hotel

Company, a subsidiary of the Great Northern that had been formed to operate the hotels, bought one other major hotel in the park in 1930. That was the Lewis Hotel, located on the west side of the park on Lake McDonald.

For the next thirty years the company owned and operated the lodges in Glacier National Park, and although they built several other modern lodges, none met the high standards established by the first group built between 1911 and 1927.

While the railroads were important to the lodges of Glacier, highways—or the lack of them—became just as important as tourists began to visit the park. Even today there are fewer than 250 miles of roads in and around the park, and most of those were built after the hotels were in place.

Fifty miles of those roads are the Roosevelt Highway, U.S. Highway 2, that runs along the southern boundary of the park and connects East and West glaciers. This highway was opened in 1930; prior to that there was not a year-round road across the Continental Divide for a hundred miles north or south of the Greatest Northern Railroad right-of-way on which the highway was constructed. The increase in automobile traffic, which had to be shipped by rail between East and West glaciers until 1930, put pressure on the government to construct several east-west routes across the divide in and near the park.

The second east-west route to open was the Going-to-the-Sun Highway, which traverses the park from its western entrance fifty-one miles to St. Mary's on its eastern boundary. Although this route opened in 1935 after an expenditure of $3 million pre-inflation depression money, the original surveys for it were made in 1916 and construction begun in 1921.

Anyone who travels the road today can quickly understand the huge cost and long construction time, for sections of the road had to be carved out of granite cliffs.

The last east-west route to open in the park was the Chief Mountain International Highway, which goes from Babb, Montana, to Waterton, Alberta. This route is forty miles long and replaced a route that required visitors going from Glacier National Park to Waterton Lakes National Park to drive north into Canada to Cardston, and then back down to Waterton, a total of over sixty miles from Babb.

These three highways were the final touch to developing easy contact among the four major hotels in the Waterton-Glacier International Peace Park. They connected the Blackfeet Highway, running for fifty miles along the eastern boundary of the park, with the western entrance to the park at Apgar.

One of the few "Grand Tours" to be offered in our national parks developed in Glacier to take advantage of the few roads. The tour began in the thirties, and still exists today. An important aspect of that tour was—and still is—the fleet of touring buses the Glacier Park Hotel Company had built to their specifications by the White Motor Company between 1936 and 1938. These oversized cars carried twelve to fourteen passengers, plus luggage, and were used to transport guests from lodge to lodge across the limited roads of Glacier National Park. In good weather, which is infrequent in some summers, the canvas tops of the buses were rolled back so passengers could have a better view of the scenic grandeur of the park.

Although the buses were built by the White Motor Company, they were painted bright red, and soon became known as the "Reds" by both tourists and company employees.

Many of the early drivers of the buses were inexperienced, particularly on narrow mountain roads, and they often jammed the gears of the buses when they downshifted on curves as they traversed the park on the Going-to-the-Sun Highway. The drivers became known as "Jammers" because of these miscues, and that name is still used today, along with "Reds."

There are thirty-two Reds left in Glacier today, still used by the lodges to transport guests from hotel to hotel on tours. Today's Jammers are more than just drivers, however, for they also act as tour guides, giving a running account of the natural and human histories of the park as they drive the guests across the passes in the Reds.

Guests can begin their "Grand Tour" of Glacier National Park from either of two starting points. One is East Glacier, where the Glacier Park Lodge is located, and the other is Apgar, at the western entrance of the 1-million acre Waterton-Glacier International Peace Park, where the Lake McDonald Lodge is located.

Although Glacier and Waterton are two separately administered parks, they were officially joined in 1932 to make the first international park in the world. This move was initiated by the Rotary Clubs of the United States and Canada, and was formally approved by both the Congress of the United States and the Parliament of Canada.

The Grand Tour includes both parks, and with fewer than 250 miles of road in and around them, tourists can actually get a better perspective of the parks by touring in the Reds than they can by traveling in private vehicles.

The real wonders of the parks are seen by walking, and guests are free to do as much of that as they want at all the lodges.

Visitors entering the parks from the east enter at East Glacier, and their first stop is the Glacier Park Lodge.

GLACIER PARK LODGE

Not only is Glacier Park Lodge the first of the great lodges on
[21] the Grand Tour when you enter the park from the east, it was also the first of the lodges built by Louis Hill in the park.

The lodge was built just outside the boundary of the park in 1912 on land Hill purchased from the Blackfeet Indians. Construction began on the hotel that summer, and it took a crew of seventy-five men a year and a half to complete the two major buildings of the lodge.

The main section, which houses the lobby, dining room, and sixty-one guest rooms, was built in 1912–13 and was opened to

The long hallway between the main lodge and the annex is an excellent place to sit on a rainy day.

The massive "forest" lobby of the Glacier Park Lodge still overwhelms the first-time guest.

guests on June 15, 1913. The annex, which housed 111 more rooms, was completed the following winter.

Although the annex wasn't completed when the lodge opened in 1913, the main building was an impressive structure by itself. Louis Hill had seen the forestry building, at the Portland Exposition of 1912, and asked architect S.L. Bartlett of Chicago to pattern the lobby of the Glacier Park Lodge after it. That wasn't an easy task, for the forestry building had been constructed of huge timbers from the forests of Oregon and Washington, and there were no such timbers available in the Montana forests around

Glacier. Hill insisted on the design, however, and had sixty immense timbers, all from trees between 500 and 800 years old, shipped from Oregon and Washington to use in the building. These timbers were all fifty-two feet long, thirty-six to forty-two inches in diameter, and weighed up to 15 tons—so big that only two at a time could be placed on flatcars for shipping to the construction site.

All sixty of the timbers were used in the construction without any modification, even the bark was left on, and you can see
[23] them today as you enter the building. The timbers in the lobby were all Douglas fir, and those used on the veranda were cedar.

The huge beams in the ceiling, the exposed girders, and even the counters at the registration desk were all carved from similar timbers that had to be cut down to size.

When the Blackfeet Indians saw the timbers being hauled in for the lobby they were so impressed they named the lodge *Oom-Cov-La-Mush*, which roughly translates into "Big Tree Lodge" or "Great Log Lodge."

When Glacier Park opened on June 15, 1913, the first guests weren't visitors who happened to show up on opening day. Instead, they were part of Louis Hill's biggest publicity stunt, and he was known for his efforts. Rather than just invite some dignitaries to help celebrate the opening of this great new lodge, Hill decided he wanted something more memorable.

Louis' father, James J. Hill, celebrated his seventy-fifth birthday in 1913, and Louis decided to hold a seventy-fifth-birthday anniversary party as the opening of the lodge. He invited all of his father's famous friends, and every engineer, conductor, brakeman, fireman, and stationmaster who had worked for the Great Northern for over twenty-five years, to the party. All of those who attended the celebration were loaded onto a special train that carried them all the way to the log railroad station that still stands in East Glacier. This station is within easy walking distance of the lodge, and the guests were quickly ensconced in the new lodge where the celebrating began in earnest.

There they enjoyed a great feast in luxury and comfort. It isn't easy to find a place large enough to comfortably seat 600 rowdy men for a feast, but the "forest" lobby of the Glacier Park Lodge was more than adequate for the occasion. This grand opening, and the accompanying celebration, became so famous that old-time railroad men from Montana to Minnesota still talk about James J.'s seventy-fifth.

If not forgotten, the opening events were quickly pushed to the background as other guests came—as many as the lodge could handle, for with the slogan Hill developed for his promotion of Glacier and his new lodges—See America First—thousands of people came to see the wonders of Glacier National Park and the lobby of the new lodge.

These visitors saw more than the park and the lobby, though. They also saw Blackfeet Indians close up. In the early years after the lodge opened a group of Blackfeet pitched teepees on the grounds in front of the lodge, and they met visitors as they disembarked from their long train journey. This impressed visitors, who still envisioned western Montana as wild Indian country, and the tribal dances that were given, sometimes even before the guests were registered, added to that feeling.

Inside the lodge the image was developed even farther. A teepee that was reputed to have once been used as the Great Council Lodge of the Blackfeet was set up on the second floor gallery, and Indian arts and crafts were exhibited throughout the lodge.

Glacier Park Lodge no longer overwhelms guests with its Indian motif—a pitch-and-putt golf course is now located where the Blackfeet used to pitch their teepees—but it stills offers a relaxing stay.

It lies just to the west of the rolling plains of the Blackfeet Reservation in western Montana and sits on the eastern base of a hundred-mile stretch of the Rocky Mountains that forms the Continental Divide inside Glacier National Park.

As the first stop on the Grand Tour on the east side of the park, it is also the gateway to the Waterton Lakes National Park in Canada. It's appropriate that you reach Waterton Lakes National Park by first stopping at the Glacier Park Lodge, for it was one of two lodges in the parks that were intimately involved in the movement to form the Waterton-Glacier International Peace Park. The other lodge is the Prince-of-Wales Hotel.

The first meeting to push for the peace park was held at the Prince-of-Wales in 1931, and the dedication of the park was held at the Glacier Park Lodge on June 9, 1932, when over 2,000 people gathered to celebrate this historic move by the U.S. and Canada.

While all the lodges in the park can be reached by road, only Glacier Park Lodge and Lake McDonald Lodge are close to Amtrak stations, and only Glacier Park Lodge is within walking distance of one.

While Glacier Park Lodge was being built on the east side of Glacier National Park, an old hunting lodge was being expanded into a major hotel on the west side. That was the Lewis Hotel, which was to be purchased by the Glacier Park Hotel Company in later years and renamed the Lake McDonald Lodge.

This is now the first stop on the Grand Tour when you enter the park from the west, and Lake McDonald Lodge sits on the shore of Lake McDonald, eleven miles from the Amtrak station in Belton.

With easy access to the park from railroad stations on both the east and west sides of the park, Glacier is the only one of the parks in this book that remains accessible by rail to all visitors who would like to use this old way of visiting the national parks.

LAKE McDONALD LODGE

Lake McDonald was a neutral stopping-off point for early mountaineers and hunters who were heading for the backcountry in what is now Glacier National Park. For those heading over Logan Pass, it was the last rest stop, the last place to get provisions before entering the wilderness.

Lake McDonald is the largest—and most accessible—lake in Glacier, and there has been commercial development around it since the late 1880s. The Great Northern Railway arrived in Belton, three miles to the south of the west end of the lake, in 1891, and resorts soon sprang up all around the lake. Most of these were built at Apgar on the west end of the lake, but one resort was completed on the east end in 1895. This was the Snyder Hotel, the first of several buildings to be located where the present Lake McDonald Lodge sits.

It wasn't easy to get to the Snyder Hotel, for there were no roads around the lake in the early 1900s, and all guests had to either travel by horse around the lake or cross it on one of the ferries that operated then. The latter became the most popular way of reaching the Snyder Hotel, but as more and more visitors went to the hotel the need for a road around the lake became obvious.

One was completed in 1913, and J.E. Lewis, who had purchased the Snyder Hotel in 1906, expanded the lodge during the winter of 1913–14 to accommodate the increasing number of visitors. The new building had sixty-five rooms in the main lodge and sixteen cabins. The lodge was an alpine-style building that followed much the same design as the Glacier Park Lodge that

Louis Hill was building on the east side of the park at the same time. Whether this was intentional, or by accident, is difficult to determine. It probably was intentional because the alpine style was in vogue at the time.

Although Lewis' lodge had the same basic design as Glacier Park Lodge, it didn't approach the tremendous size of Glacier. Instead, it gave, and gives, its guests an intimate feeling—more of the feeling of staying at an old hunting lodge than entering a forest, as the lobby of Glacier Park Lodge gives. This intimate feeling is something that the other lodges in Glacier National Park lack. They are all obviously large lodges built in the wilderness, while Lake McDonald Lodge is a smaller, more intimate structure that fits into the wilderness.

Not that the lodge doesn't have a grandeur about it. Its lobby, although small by comparison with those of Glacier Park Lodge and Many Glacier Hotel, does rise three stories, and it does have large timbers that reach to the rafters. These timbers are heavy, red cedar logs that are still wrapped in their bark, and they offer

Even the size and location of the entrance to the Lodge is more intimate than the other lodges in Glacier. There could be no better place to sit on a warm summer's evening to rest and relax.

Mounted animal heads and skins adorn the log pillars in the lobby (left) and on the upper balconies of the lodge (right).

a feeling of closeness, whereas the Glacier Park Lodge lobby gives more of a feeling of a large open forest.

The expected large fireplace lines the front wall of the lobby, but it appears huge in this lobby. It isn't dwarfed by the size of the surrounding room. On the hearth, and in the concrete floor of the lobby, are many Indian words written in the wet cement when the lodge was constructed. These add to the feeling of a private hunting lodge.

The huge fireplace, Indian words in the cement floor, and the many pelts and stuffed animal heads that hang from the red cedar pillars give the lodge the hunting-club atmosphere that seems out of place on the Grand Tour, but the dining room and veranda give a very different feel, one that is more appropriate for the Grand Tour.

The lodge sits within a hundred feet of Lake McDonald's shoreline, and the large dining room, veranda, and lounge all overlook the grassy slope leading down to the lake. The lake stretches out from the shoreline to distant peaks that reflect the late afternoon sun. On a warm summer's evening nothing could feel more like being on a Grand Tour than sitting in the handmade chairs on the veranda, sipping a drink from the lounge, and watching the colors of the peaks change as the sun drops below the horizon.

A cool breeze generally comes in off the lake as the sun disappears and drives guests inside, but inside it is just as impressive. The dining room is long, with a low ceiling, and the lake side is completely covered with windows that give an unimpeded view of the lake and distant peaks.

From the veranda and dining room it isn't hard to imagine that you are on a Grand Tour of a distant and exotic paradise. In fact, you don't have to dream this, for you can actually be on such a tour, for Glacier is exotic, and there is a Grand Tour. If you have chosen to take that tour your next stop will be the largest of the lodges and hotels in the Waterton-Glacier Park, the "Showplace of the Rockies," the Many Glacier Hotel.

THE MANY GLACIER HOTEL

On the Grand Tour of Glacier National Park, guests are transported from lodge to lodge on the Reds, and as they disembark under the porte-cochere at the Many Glacier Hotel there is little doubt as to why Louis Hill advertised it as the "Showplace of the Rockies" when it was completed in 1915. It was more than a publicist's hyperbole.

The Many Glacier Hotel was the largest of the lodges constructed by Hill in Glacier, and it was the largest hotel in Montana when it was completed. In addition, it was built in an unsurpassed natural setting. Swiftcurrent Lake, where it sits, is the largest of a series of four lakes that are ancient basins carved out as glaciers moved over soft rock. Over time the depressions left by the glaciers filled, and today the four lakes formed extend seven miles from the foot of Swiftcurrent Pass to the Many Glacier Hotel.

Not only are the lakes beautiful, they are surrounded by ridges and peaks that give guests of the Many Glacier Hotel a 360-degree panorama of natural beauty.

Louis Hill couldn't have found a site in Glacier National Park to build a lodge that would have given guests a better view of the grandeur of the park. He could have found an easier site for a hotel, though, for Swiftcurrent Valley was miles—fifty miles—from the nearest railhead and nearest good road. When construction began on the Many Glacier Hotel in the spring of
[29] 1914 there was a road of sorts leading into Swiftcurrent Lake, but it was primitive at best.

Hill had selected the site where he wanted to build the Many Glacier Hotel even before Glacier was designated as a park, and he knew that he had to build a road before he could begin construction of the lodge. With that in mind he had contracted with the Department of the Interior to build a road along the east side of the park in 1911. This road was the beginning of the

"Reds" sit in waiting at the porte-cochere of the hotel to take guests to their next stop on the Grand Tour of Glacier.

Blackfeet Highway that runs along the eastern boundary of the park today.

By the spring of 1914 the road from East Glacier was graded, but unsurfaced. That was enough to begin construction of the hotel, but not enough to keep the contractor from having a multitude of problems stemming from poor access to the site.

The graded road was sufficient to travel over in a light rig, but just barely. The contractor's problem was that he had to bring in tons of heavy equipment over the road all the way from East Glacier. That was fifty miles, and the road was almost destroyed by the time he had skidded the machinery over it.

To add to the problems with the road conditions, the huge timbers that now stand in the lobby of the Many Glacier Hotel also had to be skidded over the road from the railroad at East Glacier. The moderate-sized timbers used in the hotel were logged

The copper hood and chimney rise four stories from the first floor lobby of the Many Glacier Hotel.

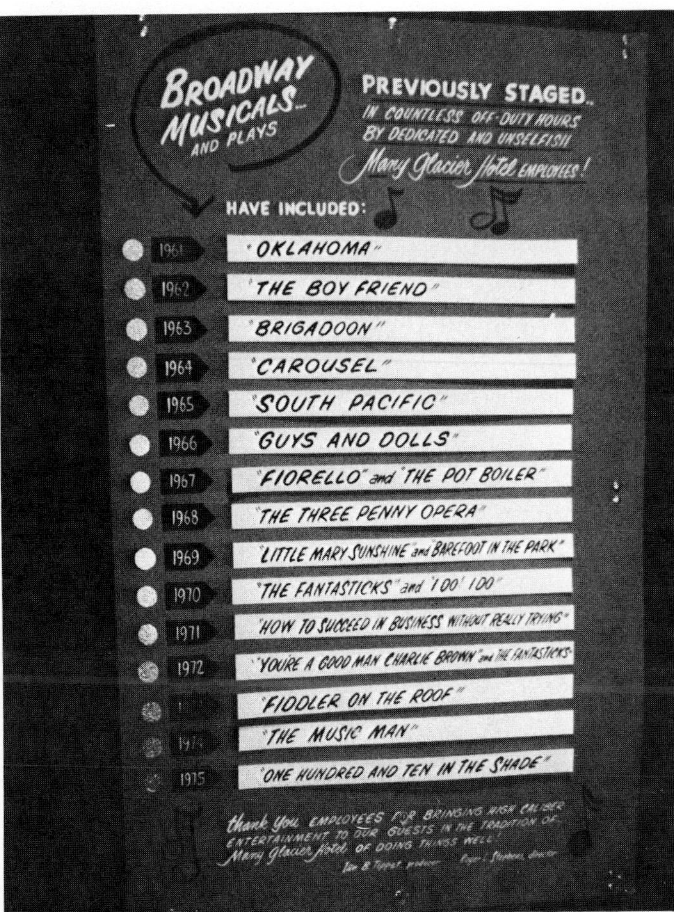

Some guests are content to play cards while being stood over by a stuffed mountain sheep, while others try to view live ones outside the hotel (left). Some of the musical comedies that have been produced at the Many Glacier Hotel over the years (right).

from Grinnell Valley up from Swiftcurrent Lake, but the large timbers were brought in from Oregon and Washington, as were those used in the Glacier Park Lodge.

A sawmill, planing mill, and temporary kiln were all set up at the construction site to mill the timbers from Grinnell Valley, and the lumber from these mills was used to build the frame, siding, and most of the furniture of the hotel. Items such as window sashes, door frames, and doors, all of which had to be made to close tolerance, were freighted in, however, for the crew didn't have the equipment available on site to make them. The massive stones that were used in the foundation and huge fireplaces were all quarried near the site.

The completed hotel was impressive. After the annex was added in 1917 the hotel ran 900 feet along the shore of

Swiftcurrent Lake. The various units of the hotel were connected so as to curve to match the shoreline of the lake.

Outside, the four stories of the hotel are dwarfed by the peaks that surround it—although at a distance—but guests are awed by the lobby as they enter the hotel. Giant pillars rise four stories, unobstructed, to a ceiling with large exposed beams and bright skylights.

The skylights give the hotel lobby an airy and open feeling, and show off the most unusual fireplace in any of the Glacier lodges. On the west end of the lobby there is a large square hearth that sits in the middle of the lobby, a four-story high copper flue with a movable hood hanging above it.

A quick tour of the interior of the hotel shows why it took 400 men working day and night almost five months to complete the main structure. The building is huge, and the finish work is outstanding. Even the exterior trim—befitting a Swiss chalet—was handcarved of native wood.

The early Indian motif of the hotel has completely disappeared, and the hotel is now strictly Alpine. Shields of Swiss cantons decorate the doors of the rooms, and the staff dresses in lederhosen and dirndls.

Louis Hill took a risk building his "Showplace of the Rockies" in such an inaccessible location, but it was a risk that paid off. Guests came to the Many Glacier Hotel in large numbers, even in the early years when the road from East Glacier was so bad that some of the tour buses had to spend as much time off the road as on it when transporting tourists from the Glacier Park Lodge to the Many Glacier Hotel.

The bad roads didn't keep guests away in the early years, and even more came after the roads were hard-surfaced between 1926 and 1929. By then last remnants of the mills that had been erected on the hotel site had been removed, but only after a show of strength by the first director of the National Park Service, Stephen Mather.

Mather had been concerned that the mills had not all been removed because the sawmill sat in full view of the hotel less than half a mile south of it. Louis Hill had delayed removing the sawmill in particular, for his local manager wanted to mill more lumber. Mather had agreed to a brief stay and emphasized that the mill would have to come down shortly.

It was still standing when Mather visited the Many Glacier Hotel in August 1925, however, and Mather decided that he had to let Hill know who was really running the parks. For too long the railroads were almost uncontrolled, and Mather knew that he had to exert his power before they would recognize the authority of the recently strengthened National Park Service.

To this end he collected several NPS work crews and gave them orders. He then invited all the hotel guests outside for what he called a demonstration. When the crowd had gathered Mather personally set off the first of thirteen dynamite charges he had instructed the work crews to place in and around the sawmill.

[33] When people in the crowd asked Mather what was going on he facetiously replied, "Celebrating my daughter's birthday." It *was* her nineteenth birthday, but Mather was very aware that the demonstration was a show of strength, as was Louis Hill when he heard of the incident. There was little Hill could do about the mill, for Mather had the legal right to do as he had, but the relations between the two were cool at best afterwards.

A decade after the roads into Many Glacier were hard-surfaced the hotel was almost destroyed by a forest fire that consumed that chalets built on the slopes of Mt. Altyn and thirty-one cabins of the Swiftcurrent Motor Lodge across Swiftcurrent Lake from the Many Glacier Hotel.

The fire began in the Heaven's Peak area in mid-August 1936 and burned for twelve days before it moved across Swiftcurrent Pass and down Swiftcurrent Valley toward the Many Glacier Hotel. One observer stated, "The hotel was only saved by heroic measures, with men posted upon its roof with wet brooms ready to extinguish any flying embers that might sail across the lake."

A shift in the winds helped firefighters stop the spread of the fire, and the Many Glacier Hotel was saved. Saved to remain one of the outstanding examples of the old lodges of our national parks. Today's guests can easily understand why Mrs. Frank Oastler spent a record 1197 days in the lodges of Glacier National Park, most of them in the Many Glacier Hotel.

This is a record that will never be matched, for most guests today come to the lodges on tours, and seldom stay more than a night or two. That's too bad, for there are many activities in Glacier to occupy guests for much longer periods. There is even nightly entertainment at all of the lodges as was common in most lodges in the national parks in the early years. Lodges in most other parks have discontinued their nightly entertainment, although some offer occasional skits by staff.

While the entertainment at the Glacier Park Lodge and Lake McDonald is low-keyed, and is often no more than supervised square dancing, that offered at the Many Glacier Hotel is noted for its professional quality.

Competition is tough for all summer jobs in the lodges in Glacier—as many as 15,000 applications are filed each year for fewer than 900 positions—but it is even more so for positions at the Many Glacier Hotel. To get a job as a busboy, a maid, or a clerk at the Many Glacier young applicants not only have to pass a personal interview, they also have to pass a musical talent competition.

That is because Ian Tippet, who is both personnel director for Glacier Park, Inc., and manager of the Many Glacier Hotel, has developed a tradition during his years at Many Glacier. A tradition of having a staff that performs first-class musical programs for the guests. Some members of the staff form a mini-symphony orchestra, some form choral groups, and others form instrumental and vocal groups. These rotate performances throughout the week all during the summer, and then participate in the most unusual activity. That is the professional presentation of at least one light opera or musical comedy production each summer.

All of the musical presentations are in addition to regular jobs for all the staff, and they get no extra pay for the productions. What they get is the experience. The guests are the ones who get the extra, for no other lodge in the national parks offers anything comparable.

There is much more to do at the Many Glacier Hotel than listen to music, though, for the hotel sits in one of the most scenic parts of Glacier National Park. Peaks that form part of the Continental Divide surround the hotel, and a short hike takes guests into unspoiled wilderness where many types of wildlife, including grizzlies and mountain sheep, can be spotted.

Sometimes guests at Many Glacier don't have to walk any further than outside the hotel to enjoy wildlife that one generally associates with inaccessible mountain craigs. Nowhere else in the national parks do you find signs that read "Please Do Not Feed the Mountain Sheep." Although their appearances are infrequent, mountain sheep do occasionally come down from the higher peaks surrounding Swiftcurrent Lake to visit the saltlick that is located near the Many Glacier Hotel.

On some nights guests don't even have to leave the hotel to encounter Glacier's wildlife. Over the years a number of bats have made the loft of the hotel their homes, and, since the hotel is in a national park where wildlife is protected, the management is not allowed to kill or disturb the bats. This proves a distraction to some guests who stay on the top floor—but at least it is the hotel that has bats in its belfry, and not the guests.

Many Glacier Hotel was the last great hotel that Louis Hill built in Glacier National Park, but he did build one other hotel nearby. That one was on a knoll that juts out into Waterton Lake with a view south toward the northern boundary of Glacier National Park.

[35]

PRINCE-OF-WALES HOTEL

The Prince-of-Wales stands as a sentinel over Waterton Lake.

Louis Hill chose the site where he wanted to build the Prince-of-Wales Hotel in 1913, but it took him until 1926 to convince the Canadian government to lease him the land. The spot he had chosen was a promontory 100 feet higher than the northern end of Waterton Lake. This promontory offered a full view of the lake and the peaks of the Continental Divide that continued across the U.S.-Canadian border into Glacier National Park.

Hill had originally planned a hotel similar to the Many Glacier Hotel, with three stories spread out around a large central lobby, and containing 200 rooms. The completed structure had little resemblance to the original design, for Hill changed his mind several times during construction. That, combined with one of

The fine woodwork and wallpaper make the Prince-of-Wales' interior far from rustic.

The columns supporting the second floor are small in contrast to the immense log pillars in the other hotels and lodges in Glacier.

the worst winters ever experienced at Waterton, caused the contractor innumerable problems.

Construction began on the hotel during the summer of 1926, but work bogged down quickly. The nearest railhead was thirty miles away at Cardston, Alberta, and there were no improved roads into Waterton. Everyone had miscalculated how long it would take to get the boilers and other heavy equipment to the site, and winter had set in by the time everything was set up for construction to begin in earnest.

The next six months brought severe weather, and that, along with Hill's constantly changing mind, almost brought the construction to a total halt. Some portions of the hotel were actually rebuilt four times because Hill changed his mind about the design. And these were not minor changes of mind. What had begun as a long, three-story building turned into a tall—seven stories tall—rectangular building.

As the building was being rebuilt high winds rose at the site. Winds so strong that the contractor feared he would not be able to complete the project. He continued only after the wind velocities were declared safe by anemometer measurements. They may have been declared safe, but that doesn't mean they were calm, for twice during the construction the building was blown off center by high winds. Construction had gone so far the second time that the building could not be realigned, and the upper stories of the hotel are still out of plumb with the lower stories.

The high winds didn't stop when the hotel was completed, and today's guests, particularly those on the top floors, can feel the building move during heavy winds. There is no danger in this movement, however, for the contractor was well aware of the problems of the high winds and built the hotel to withstand the severest gales.

The changes made by Hill during the construction caused delays and tripled the cost of the building, but the Prince-of-Wales opened its doors to guests on July 25, 1927. The drastic change in plans, high winds, severe winter, and ever-present bears were all obstacles to successfully completing the hotel, but none of these is obvious in the finished product. The Prince-of-Wales Hotel, named after the future Edward VIII (legend has it that he attended the opening ceremonies but the records show that he didn't), is a facility worthy of its name. Its seven stories are dwarfed by the surrounding peaks, and the view offered to its guests over the entire length of Waterton Lake, with Glacier National Park visible in the distance across the longest unguarded international border in the world, is unmatched.

Four years after the Prince-of-Wales opened, Rotary Clubs from Montana and Alberta held a meeting there, and it was at that meeting that the idea for the formation of an international peace park that included both the Waterton National Park and Glacier National Park was first proposed. The resolution passed by the Rotarians on July 4, 1931, was later approved by the U.S. Congress and the Canadian Parliament. The park was dedicated the following year at the Glacier Park Lodge.

The Prince-of-Wales was closed from 1933 until 1936 because of the Great Depression, and again from 1941 until 1946 because of World War II, but has been open every summer since.

Although it is closed during the winter months, the residents of Waterton have been thankful twice since World War II for Louis Hill's choice of site for the Prince-of-Wales. In 1964 and again in 1975 the low-lying town of Waterton had to be evacuated because of flood waters, and both times the townspeople used the hotel as

Furnace Creek Inn, Death Valley National Monument.

Furnace Creek Inn, Death Valley National Monument (both pages).

Furnace Creek Inn, Death Valley National Monument (both pages).

Glacier Park Lodge, Glacier National Park.

Lake McDonald Lodge, Glacier National Park.

One of the Reds that serve the lodges in Glacier National Park (top). Many Glacier Hotel, Glacier National Park (above).

Many Glacier Hotel, Glacier National Park (top).
Prince-of-Wales Hotel, Glacier National Park (above).

Prince-of-Wales Hotel, Glacier National Park (opposite).
El Tovar, Grand Canyon National Park (this page).

El Tovar, Grand Canyon National Park.

El Tovar, Grand Canyon National Park (top).
Bright Angel Lodge, Grand Canyon National Park (above).

Bright Angel Lodge, Grand Canyon National Park.

Bright Angel Lodge, Grand Canyon National Park (top).
Wonderland Club Hotel, Great Smoky Mountains National Park (above).

Wonderland Club Hotel, Great Smoky Mountains National Park.

a center of rescue operations, and for temporary housing, until the waters receded.

The Prince-of-Wales is the only hotel in this book that isn't in a U.S. national park, but it is included as part of the Grand Tour of the Waterton-Glacier International Peace Park offered by Glacier Park, Inc., and has many historical ties with other lodges in the park that were also constructed by Louis Hill and the Great Northern Railway.

Grand Canyon National Park

RAILROADS AND NATIONAL PARKS—THE TWO SEEMED TO HAVE BEEN almost inseparable in the early days of the national parks, and the development of the lodges at Grand Canyon was no exception. The difference there was that the most famous of the hotels in the park was built by the Santa Fe Railway almost fifteen years before the canyon was designated a national park.

Commercial interests began to promote tourism at the south rim of the Grand Canyon as early as the 1880s, but the area remained isolated and difficult to reach until after 1900. Before then the only way to reach the canyon other than by walking or horseback was by stage coach, and that entailed an eleven-hour ride over a trail that was hot and dusty in summer and cold and muddy in winter.

So few tourists made the effort to visit the canyon by stage that there was only one hotel at the south rim as late as 1900, and it was quite small. This changed on September 18, 1901, when the Santa Fe Railway officially opened a branch line running from Williams, Arizona, to the south rim near the old Bright Angel Hotel.

The Bright Angel was soon overflowing with guests, and an early settler of the Grand Canyon, Ralph Cameron, opened a second hotel. He built the Cameron Hotel on an old mining claim that lay between the railroad terminal and the Bright Angel Hotel, which had been purchased by the Santa Fe. This meant that all disembarking passengers had to pass by the Cameron Hotel before they reached the Bright Angel. The Santa Fe was unhappy about this, but the only thing they could do was move their terminal. This is what they did. After they extended the railway several hundred feet to the east, all passengers had to pass by the Bright Angel first.

Santa Fe was too powerful for Cameron to compete with, and

he was forced to close his hotel when the Santa Fe opened the first major hotel on the south rim of the Grand Canyon.

EL TOVAR

The Santa Fe began plans for their new luxury hotel at the south rim soon after they began work on the branch line that would take guests to it. They asked architect Charles Whittlesey
[41] to design them a hotel that would combine the best features of a Swiss chateau and a Rhine castle, and would be built of native stones and logs.

The completed hotel was a long, rambling building that used large native boulders to set off the pine logs from Oregon, and it was built on a site that offered a vertigo-inducing view of the 6,000-foot vertical drop to the bottom on Grand Canyon. Guests could gaze from there at the north rim over the thirteen-mile chasm that stretched out from the hotel site.

In its original state after it opened in 1905, the lodge fit simply and naturally into the surrounding landscape of boulders and pinon pine. This natural setting has been disrupted over the years as other buildings have been erected around the lodge, but the view from the balconies and porches of El Tovar have remained unimpeded. In its stately splendor, El Tovar remains the dominant building in Grand Canyon Village.

In a brochure published by the Santa Fe in 1909, El Tovar was said to be more like a big country club than the Waldorf-Astoria, and that is still true. You enter the hotel, not through a porte-cochere, but through a large porch built of stone and pine logs. The first room you enter is the Rendezvous Room, a forty-one-foot by thirty-seven-foot public room whose bulky rafters and dark log walls seem to absorb the unrelenting Arizona sun. The enclosed feeling of the lobby and Rendezvous Room give way to a bright and open feeling as you move down white hallways whose walls are decorated with handdrawn Indian designs, and into rooms that all receive direct sunlight sometime during the day.

In the beginning, as today El Tovar was run by the Fred Harvey Company. Harvey had begun his close association with the Atchison, Topeka, and the Santa Fe in 1876 when he began to operate the railway's restaurants and hotels. By 1905, when El Tovar opened, Fred Harvey was dead, but his sons continued to run the company as an integral part of the Santa Fe Railway system.

They were already operating several luxury hotels for the

A single guest stands on his private balcony to view the changing colors of the Grand Canyon in early morning.

Santa Fe, and the service and conveniences they offered guests at El Tovar in those early years made it one of the most luxurious hotels in the country. "Harvey girls," dressed in starched-black dresses, served guests in a dining room that had silverware, fine china, and crystal set on exquisite linen.

The food matched the setting. The best meat and produce was brought in daily on Santa Fe trains; the milk, cheese, and butter all came from the Harvey Company's own dairy herd at the hotel; the eggs came from hens kept with the dairy herd; and—in later years—the fresh flowers on the tables came from a greenhouse built at Grand Canyon Village.

Add the Grand Canyon and you had a most unusual luxury hotel. Some guests seemed to think that the canyon was the addition, rather than El Tovar. John Burroughs, the famous naturalist, claimed to have heard one woman guest exclaim, in all seriousness, "They built the canyon too near this beautiful hotel."

El Tovar wasn't the first building that the Fred Harvey Company opened at the south rim. The company had become active

Six suites have private balconies where guests can sit in solitude while they view the canyon beyond.

in resurrecting the native arts and crafts of the Southwest Indians, and had hired Mary Jane Colter in 1902 to decorate the Indian Building they had erected next to their new Alvarado Ho-

All guests can view the deep chasm of the canyon a few steps from the porch of El Tovar.

The walls of the halls are decorated with hand-drawn Indian designs.

tel in Albuquerque. That enterprise was such a success they decided to construct a similar structure next to El Tovar.

Colter was retained to design and supervise the construction of what is now known as Hopi House. She used a replica of an actual unit of homes from the Hopi village of Oraibi in her design of Hopi House, and today the building houses a gift shop specializing in Southwest Indian arts and crafts. When Hopi House opened in 1905, several months before El Tovar, it also housed Indians. Instead of just bringing in arts and crafts from the reservations, Colter decided to bring in native craftspeople, and let El Tovar guests see the arts and crafts being produced.

For a number of years Hopi and Navajo families lived in and around Hopi House as they made their wares, and sold them to the tourists.

Hopi House was only the first of six public buildings that Mary Jane Colter was to design and build for Fred Harvey in the next thirty years. In those years she designed the Lookout Studio, Hermit's Rest, Phantom Ranch, the Watchtower, and Bright Angel Lodge.

Of those buildings, only Phantom Ranch and Bright Angel Lodge were lodges, but the other three structures are worthy of note. Lookout Studio was built by the Santa Fe in 1914 after they had attempted to remove the Kolb brothers from their studio at the head of the Bright Angel Trail. The Kolbs refused to sell out to Santa Fe, and then faced the same kind of pressure the company had put on Ralph Cameron a decade earlier.

If they couldn't remove the Kolbs, Santa Fe felt they could at least outmaneuver them. To that end they had Mary Colter design a studio that would sit on the rim of the canyon between El

Tovar and the Kolb studio that would draw customers away from the Kolbs.

Colter designed a building to fit in with the rock surroundings that was unobtrusive, made of native stone, and with an exterior that made it almost invisible to those not looking for it. The rugged outline of the roof molded in so well with the edge of the rim that hikers on the Bright Angel Trail below were unable to see the building.

The natural design of the Lookout Studio was an example of
[45] the buildings Colter was to design for the Grand Canyon area in the following two decades, buildings that fit in so well with the environment that the NPS soon followed her lead in designing their own buildings.

The same year that the Lookout was opened Colter completed another building for Fred Harvey. This was a rest stop that was constructed at the end of the rim road some eight miles to the west of El Tovar. The Harvey Company had just spent $185,000 to build this road and wanted a place where passengers on their touring stages could rest and have refreshments.

Several designs were considered by the company, most of the same alpine style as El Tovar. Colter's primitive-stonework style won, however, and she built a structure that looked like a jumble of stones from the outside, and which looked so old on the inside that some Santa Fe employees asked her why she didn't clean it up before it was opened to the public.

Beartraps, and irons that could have come from a medieval castle, exposed log beams, and a fireplace alcove all gave the finished building the appearance of having been built by an untrained mountain man.

Colter's next project for Fred Harvey at the Grand Canyon was about as far away from the rim as you could get. It was on the bottom on the canyon itself.

For several years there had been guests who wanted to see the more isolated north rim of the canyon, and in 1907 David Rust, who operated a hunting camp on the north rim, built a cable across the Colorado River at the end of the Bright Angel Trail. A tram car was attached to this cable to transport adventurous guests across the Colorado so they could hike out to the north rim.

After Grand Canyon was declared a national park in 1919 the NPS decided to replace Rust's cable car with a suspension bridge. The first Kaibab Suspension Bridge was completed in 1922, and the Fred Harvey Company opened a tourist camp on Bright Angel Creek that same summer.

PHANTOM RANCH

There were two restrictions on the construction of the buildings at the Harvey tourist camp on Bright Angel Creek. The first was a NPS directive that had been released several years earlier that stated, "In construction of roads, trails and buildings and other improvements, particular attention must be devoted always to the harmonizing of these improvements with the landscape. . . ." The second was that all materials for the buildings, except for native stone that was gathered nearby, had to be brought down from the rim on pack mules.

Colter's design for the buildings at Phantom Ranch certainly fit both restrictions. Her use of uncut river boulders for the walls of the buildings, and simple sloped roofs with overhanging eaves incorporated a style that fit both restrictions. It blended in perfectly with the surroundings, and it utilized as much of the local material, boulders, as possible so that less had to be brought in on the mules.

In the decade of the twenties Phantom Ranch lost much of its desert atmosphere and became a green oasis at the bottom of the canyon. Between 1924 and 1928 new stone cottages, a recreation hall, a blacksmith shop, showers and toilets were all added to this rustic retreat. The ranch even approached self-sufficiency, as an alfalfa field for growing feed for the livestock was added near the fruit orchard that had been planted in 1918; rabbits and chickens were raised near the mule barn; and water was supplied by a reservoir that had been built above the ranch.

In its early years Phantom Ranch was frequented by so many famous guests that its guest book read like a Who's Who. Most of these guests stayed at El Tovar on the rim, then spent several days at Phantom Ranch on the bottom of the canyon, and there were constant newspaper accounts of the rich and famous visiting Grand Canyon. Because of those visits El Tovar and Phantom Ranch became well known across the country in the twenties.

A new bridge was built across the Colorado in 1928, and during the early 1930s the Civilian Conservation Corps did extensive work on the floor of the Grand Canyon, including considerable remodeling at Phantom Ranch. By 1950 the NPS began to make the area more natural and tore down some of the buildings that had been erected over the years. In 1972 the swimming pool at the ranch was filled in, and Phantom Ranch was returned to a state close to what Mary Jane Colter had envisioned when she drew the designs for it in 1922.

In 1932 Mary Colter built one of her most unusual structures along the rim on the Grand Canyon. Hermit's Rest, which she designed in 1914, had been very popular with tourists over the years, and the Harvey Company decided they needed a similar stop for tourists on the east side of El Tovar.

Colter again went to the early Southwest for her ideas. This time she went even farther back than the mountain men—she went all the way back to a time before the first Europeans came to the Southwest. Back to prehistory when the first Indians to

settle in the area built huge watchtowers of stone to help give warnings when unfriendly visitors approached.

Colter visited as many of the ruins of old watchtowers as she could find and carefully drew up plans for a recreated watchtower for the rest stop at Desert View, twenty-five miles east of El Tovar.

The finished structure was much larger than any of the prehistoric watchtowers had been—it was seventy feet tall—and had a thirty-foot diameter at the base.

The four stories of the tower contained a large observation room built in the style of a Hopi kiva on the first level, art galleries on the next two levels where guests could view outstanding examples of Indian art, and an open observation platform on the roof. This observation platform offered a panoramic view of the canyon and was at 7,522 feet, the highest spot on the south rim.

Colter had just completed the finishing touches on the Watchtower when she began her last major project for Fred Harvey at the Grand Canyon. That was the Bright Angel Lodge.

BRIGHT ANGEL LODGE

The old Bright Angel Hotel had been built by John Hance at the head of the Bright Angel Trail in the 1890s, but it had been gradually phased out by the Santa Fe Railway after El Tovar opened. There had been several plans for a moderate-priced lodge over the years—Colter had even drawn some plans for a new lodge on the site in 1916—but the Harvey Company kept delaying construction for a number of reasons.

By 1934 they were ready to complete the project, though, and had Colter draw up several new plans. All of those plans were turned down by NPS because Colter had designed them for the edge of the rim. Over the years the NPS had decided that all visitors should have an unimpeded access to the rim and would not consider any new construction that interfered with that access.

Colter's next set of plans were approved, for she had moved the proposed site away from the rim slightly and had designed a long, low lodge that would be constructed of natural woods. This building was to have shops and restaurants in addition to rooms, and a cluster of cabins was to be built adjacent to the main lodge.

Colter fought to have several of the historic buildings on the site included in the new lodge, and the main building of the Cameron Hotel, which had served as the Grand Canyon Post Office after it closed, was made into one of the cabins. The cabin where Bucky O'Neill, a colorful character of the early Grand Canyon days, had lived was included in the lodge itself.

Although the Bright Angel Lodge was built for guests who couldn't afford the more luxurious accommodations of El Tovar, Colter didn't skimp when it came to furnishing the private and public rooms. She searched throughout Arizona to find furnishings that had been brought across the desert by early Arizona settlers, and she used the many pieces she found to fill the lodge and cabins. This added an authenticity to the pioneer atmo-

Lookout Studio as seen from the patio behind Bright Angel Lodge. Both were designed by Mary Jane Colter.

sphere that Colter was attempting to create at the Bright Angel Lodge, and her desire for authenticity went beyond the pioneer atmosphere.

Colter had built a gigantic fireplace in the lobby that had a huge wooden thunderbird, or "bright angel from the sky," hanging above it. The fireplace was recessed into the rear wall of the lobby and had benches on each side where guests could warm themselves. As impressive as this huge fireplace was, and is, it had to take a back seat to the one built in the lounge. There, set between two large picture windows that overlook the canyon, Colter designed a fireplace that used stones from each major stratum of the canyon. The hearth is made of stones from the riverbed of the Colorado, and strata continue in order until a layer of Kaibab limestone finishes off the top of the ten-foot-high fireplace.

Because of the care Colter put into the design of this moderate-priced lodge it was a success from the barbecue attended by 2,000 people celebrating its opening until today. Its moderate prices helped bring back the guests who had stopped visiting the Grand Canyon during the darkest years of the Depression. Soon after Bright Angel Lodge opened in 1935 the number of visitors to the canyon exceeded the number who had come each year before the Depression.

These visitors were different from the guests who had ridden the Santa Fe for years to stay at El Tovar and to ride the mules down to Phantom Ranch. These came by car rather than by train, and they tended to stay fewer days. The Bright Angel satisfied their needs perfectly, and it continues to be the most popular lodge at the south rim today.

The Santa Fe branch line reached the rim in 1901, and the railway continued to play an important role in the life of the south rim, but it gradually lost out to the automobile. The first car reached the rim less than a year after the Santa Fe branch line opened, but it wasn't until 1926 that the number of visitors to the south rim who came by car exceeded the number who came by train.

The railway's importance to the life of the south rim declined slowly over the years, until 1968, when all rail services were suspended.

While the Santa Fe played an important role in the commercial development of the south rim, it did little to develop the north rim of the canyon. Access to the north was just too limited, and it was too far away (over 200 miles by road today) from El Tovar,

The fireplace in the lobby of the Bright Angel Lodge is a good place for guests to warm themselves.

the Bright Angel, and other Santa Fe holdings for it to be profitable for the Santa Fe to try to develop the area.

The first attempt to commercialize the north rim came in 1917, just two years before the canyon was declared a national park, when W.W. Wylie, who had operated camps in Yellowstone, opened the Wylie Way Camp. Most of the guests came from the Zion and Bryce areas of southern Utah over poor roads.

At Stephan Mather's insistence the Union Pacific Railroad began to develop lodges in Zion and Bryce. In 1923 they formed the Utah Parks Company to handle these enterprises, and in 1927 the NPS designated Utah Parks as the concessionaire for the north rim of the Grand Canyon. They immediately began construction of a first-class lodge on the rim to handle the visitors who were coming in over the road that had been completed in 1917.

GRAND CANYON LODGE

[51]

The thick stone walls of the lodge were all that stood after the lodge was gutted by fire in the 1930s.

A certain amount of snob appeal often develops around inaccessible places and things. This happened at the Grand Canyon, where the inaccessible north rim became the mecca for those who could afford the extra time and cost it took to stay there. Even though the south rim had El Tovar, a mystique developed around the less-crowded north rim that continues to this day.

Part of that mystique surrounds the Grand Canyon Lodge. This lodge was completed in 1928, a little more than a year after the Utah Parks Company was given the concession at the north rim, and it immediately became the in-place to go.

The main lodge is made of Kaibab limestone and sits directly on the north rim near Bright Angel Point. This part of the lodge rises up from the rim like a sentinel tower when viewed from Bright Angel Point, and it gives guests an impressive view of the canyon. The large picture windows of the lounge face to the south and west, allowing guests to watch the changing colors of the canyon walls as the sun sets.

On warm nights guests can get the same view from the large Kaibab-limestone-tile deck that extends out to the east of the lounge. This deck has a huge fireplace where guests can warm themselves as the evening cool descends after the sun disappears behind the distant horizon. This coolness happens almost nightly at the high elevation of the north rim during the summer, and it turns to cold as fall comes. While the lodges on the south rim are open year-round, the Grand Canyon Lodge is limited to a short summer session because of the severe winters on the rim.

The lodge houses the lounge, restaurant, and other public rooms, but guests are housed in the 120 log cabins that are spread out around the north side of the lodge away from the rim of the canyon.

The Grand Canyon Lodge was closed in 1932, not because of the Depression, which had caused many lodges in the national parks to close, but because the main lodge was gutted by fire. The walls made of huge stones still stood after the fire, but the large log beams and the shingle roof were completely burned.

The Utah Parks Company began rebuilding the lodge in the summer of 1936 and planned to work all winter to have the lodge open for the 1937 summer season. The snowfall that winter was so heavy, however, that they couldn't keep the roads open. As the snow piled higher some of the crew had to be evacuated from the rim by snow tractors, while others walked down the Kaibab Trail to Phantom Ranch, where they were given mule rides to the top

The flagstone patio behind the main lodge is an excellent place to watch the sun setting over the canyon.

On a summer evening this patio is crowded with guests as they watch the sun set. A large fire often burns in the corner fireplace.

of the south rim, which is several thousand feet lower than the north rim.

Although only ten air-miles apart, the north and south rims of the Grand Canyon are worlds apart in both appearance and atmosphere. Many more visitors come to the south rim, and there is a more hectic attitude among the guests at the lodges. Most stay for only a day or two while making a cursory tour of the rim.

Far fewer visitors come to the north rim, but those who do tend to stay longer and to be more relaxed, as they view the canyon in a more leisurely manner.

At either rim, though, guests are well aware of the presence of others; overcrowded conditions at the Grand Canyon had been foretold as early as 1938, just three years after the Fred Harvey

Company opened the Bright Angel Lodge, when visitors discovered they had to have reservations to stay at a lodge on the south rim. The NPS attempted to alleviate this overcrowding in the 1950s and 1960s by constructing several new lodges, but the increase of visitors to the park outstripped even that effort.

[54]

Closed for the winter the lodge stands silently above the canyon.

The cabins fan out from the main lodge in a park-like atmosphere.

Today El Tovar, Bright Angel, Phantom Ranch, and Grand Canyon Lodge all continue to offer first-class accommodations to a fullhouse year-round.

The Great Smoky Mountains National Park

OVER NINE MILLION VISITORS A YEAR PASS THROUGH THE GREAT SMOKY Mountains National Park, making it the most visited of our national parks, yet lodge accommodations can be said to be nonexistent within the park. The thousands of hotel and motel rooms in the small towns surrounding the park more than make up for this lack—Gatlinburg, with a population of 3,500, can house 35,000 hotel and motel guests nightly—but the Smokies lack what most of the large western parks have, a large and famous lodge.

What the park does have is too small, almost nondescript, lodges that together can house fewer than 100 guests a night. This is the least number of guest rooms in any of our major parks, but if the NPS had had its way in the 1970s there wouldn't even be these two lodges. In those years it attempted to close both down because they did not fit in with the wilderness status of the rest of the park.

Fortunately, the NPS was unsuccessful in its attempts, and both lodges were given new twenty-year leases on life. The oldest of the two lodges, the Wonderland Club Hotel, will be approaching a hundred years of age when those leases are up, and hopefully NPS policy will have changed by then so it can be designated an historic site. And an historic site it is, for it is the only remaining example of the hunting and fishing lodges that dotted the western edge of the Great Smoky Mountains in the first two decades of this century.

WONDERLAND CLUB HOTEL

A neighbor once told my wife to go ahead and put down an old oriental rug we had acquired. "After all," she said, "shabby gentility is better than no gentility at all."

[57]

The old hotel sits in the background uphill from a swing that is seldom empty on a summer day.

There couldn't be a more fitting statement about the Wonderland Club Hotel, particularly in relationship to the multitude of modern lodges that border the Great Smoky Mountains National Park. The Wonderland may be shabbier than most of the surrounding lodges, but it does have gentility. A wonderful gentility that is reminiscent of a southern hunting lodge of the twenties. And that is as it should be, for that is what the Wonderland Club was for a number of years before the Great Smoky Mountains National Park was formed. The garish surroundings of Pigeon Forge and Gatlinburg just can't compete with those memories.

No major route goes near the western edge of the Smokies, but even there the Wonderland Hotel was built because of a railroad. More than twenty years before the national park was declared in the Smokies, the Little River Lumber Company owned tracts of land in the area of Elkmont. In 1909 the company built a logging railroad into the village of Elkmont from the small town of Walland.

Since a branch line of the Southern Railway ran from Knoxville to Walland, the Little River Lumber Company soon began transporting men who wanted to visit the Elkmont area to hunt and fish.

In those years lumber companies didn't farm their cut-over land. Instead, they moved on to other virgin stands of timber. Cut-over land was considered useless to most lumber companies, but Colonel W.B. Townsend, president of the Little River Lumber Company, saw the benefits of attracting large numbers of tourists to the Elkmont area. Logging railroads were generally torn up as soon as an area was logged over, but Townsend knew that he could keep the Walland-to-Elkmont line open longer if he could keep the men from Knoxville coming to Elkmont.

To keep the hunters and fishermen coming, Townsend came up with what he considered a brilliant idea. He gave fifty acres of cut-over land to Charles B. Carter of the Wonderland Park Company, with the stipulation that he build a hotel on the land within a year.

The lobby of the hotel makes guests feel right at home with its sofa, crib, and hooked rug.

That was in 1911, and on June 1, 1912, the Wonderland Hotel opened its doors to guests, and it stayed open for the next seven years as a public hotel.

In those years so many men came to the area from Knoxville that the more affluent decided they wanted their own facility where the general public wasn't allowed. They organized, named themselves the Appalachian Club, and opened their own hotel close by the Wonderland that was open only to members and their guests.

[59] This club became so popular that it was soon turning away applicants, some of whom banded together to form a new club. Rather than build a hotel, the new club bought the Wonderland, and named themselves after it, calling their club the Wonderland Club.

They bought the Wonderland in 1919, renamed it the Wonderland Club Hotel, and closed its doors to all but members and guests. Within a year some members of the club wanted more privacy than that afforded by the main lodge, and built an annex just to the west of the main building. This annex is still owned by members of what is now the Elkmont Preservation Society under provisions of the present NPS lease.

The Wonderland Club began as a men-only hunting and fishing club, but the wives who were left in the sweltering summers of Knoxville soon heard their husbands' stories of the restful nature of the hotel and of the mild summer climate of the Smokies.

The wives' thoughts of the two-story wooden hotel built on a small hill near the Little River and of spending mild summer evening on the veranda that ran the full length of the hotel made them want a respite from the heat and humidity of Knoxville. They were soon joining their husbands at the Wonderland Club Hotel for stays that lasted from a week to a month, and the club began to add some of the amenities of the resorts that were springing up around Gatlinburg. But it never lost its hunting-club atmosphere.

In the early 1920s guests could reach the Wonderland Club by either walking or riding a horse from Gatlinburg, or by the logging train from Walland. By 1925 a narrow road was completed that ran from Gatlinbrug to Elkmont, and so many guests chose to come by automobile that the Little River Lumber Company removed their railroad in 1926.

The Appalachian Club's hotel burned down in the 1920s and was never rebuilt. Many of its members had built cabins on the small lots that were deeded to them when they joined the club,

Both sides of the double fireplace are often ablaze. The homey sitting room can be seen on the far side of the fireplace.

and the other members decided it was not worth the expense to rebuild the hotel.

Both clubs were still going strong, though, when the Great Smoky Mountains National Park was formed in 1934. The federal government began to buy out most of the private land held within the boundaries of the new park, and offered two choices to most landowners. The first choice was for the owners to receive full appraised value for their land and sign over all rights to the land to the government. The second choice was a bit more complicated. Owners who didn't want to give up control of their land could retain a lifetime lease to it in exchange for 50 percent of the appraised value of the property. Both the Appalachian and Wonderland Clubs chose the second alternative, and a list of members of the two clubs was certified by the government. The lifetime lease of the clubs for the land that included the Wonderland Club Hotel was to last until all members on the lists were dead.

In the early 1950s the remaining members of the Appalachian Club traded in their lifetime lease for a renewable twenty-year lease. That lease expired in 1972, at which time the members of the Wonderland Club joined together with those from the Appalachian Club to form the Elkmont Preservation Association. The new association received a new twenty-year lease at that time, which is still in effect.

Under this lease the Elkmont Preservation Association retains control of the Wonderland Club Hotel, with the right to lease it out to a third party.

Today, the hotel is serving guests who come to enjoy the gentility of the old hunting club in a building that is far from luxurious, as are many of the other lodges in this book. Instead, the hotel offers individuality—no two rooms are the same—and comfort. This comfort doesn't include television, radio, or telephones, however, for none of the rooms have any of these conveniences. It does offer cleanliness, although there is no doubt but that you have walked into something quite different from a Holiday Inn as you enter the lobby of the Wonderland Club Hotel. It also offers some of the finest homecooked food available in or near the park.

The old tongue-and-groove walls have been replaced with fire-resistant sheetrock, but the split-log-mantled fireplace in the dining room and the large double fireplace in the lobby still burn on cool days and evenings to give a cheery and homey atmosphere to the hotel.

You don't have to be a guest to enjoy the hospitality of the Wonderland Club Hotel, for unlike many other lodges, they extend an open invitation to park visitors to come, sit on the veranda in one of the many rocking chairs and gliders that are always there, enjoy the view of the Smokies, and listen to the quiet ripple of the Little River that is just across the road from the hotel.

The busiest time of the year for the Wonderland, and also the best time to visit the park, is in the fall when the deep colors of the Smoky Mountains' varied forests can be viewed. Guests can drive through the park, hike along the many miles of trails, or just sit on the veranda of the hotel to see these colors. When the cool of the evening drives them back to the hotel, the warmth of the fireplaces helps remove the autumn chill.

While the Wonderland is great for guests who are most content enjoying the wonders of the Smokies while sitting, the only other lodge in the park is most definitely for those who enjoy more strenuous activity, guests who have to exert themselves just to reach it.

LE CONTE LODGE

The National Park Service attempted to close down Le Conte Lodge in the 1970s because it was located in an area that had been designated as wilderness and because it was causing extensive pollution in and around its site. The interesting aspect of this move was that there may not have been a Great Smoky Mountains National Park if it had not been for Le Conte Lodge and its predecessor, Mt. Le Conte Camp.

In the 1920s a group of men in Eastern Tennessee formed the Great Smoky Mountains Conservation Association, whose pur- [62]

The cabins of the lodge overlook Gatlinburg.

The dining room isn't fancy, but no one skips a meal.

pose, as stated on its letterhead, was "the preservation of the remaining primeval forests in Eastern America and a national park in the Great Smoky Mountains."

At that time most of the land around Mt. Le Conte, including the mountain itself, was owned by the Champion Fiber Company. The company had always allowed visitors unlimited access to this peak, the highest in the Smokies, but they changed their policy in the mid 1920s when the number of visitors increased dramatically because of the publicity surrounding the Smokies and the possibility that a national park would be formed in them. Many of these new visitors didn't even know how to put out a campfire or why it should be put out. As a result of the fires and other destruction caused by the increased number of campers, Champion closed down the area around Mt. Le Conte to all except the few people who could get written permission from the company. One such group was the Great Smoky Mountains Conservation Association.

One member of that group was Paul Adams, a young naturalist who did a lot of camping on Mt. Le Conte. At Adam's suggestion the Association made a recommendation that a permanent camp be established on Mt. Le Conte where campers could stay without damaging the surrounding forest. The association asked that they be allowed to run the camp and make sure all campers observed good conservation practices.

The idea had not been approved by Champion in 1924 when the first governmental commission studying the Smokies as a potential national park visited the Mt. Le Conte area. Adams had climbed the peak with the commission and shown them the area, but there was no base camp where the group could be hosted. By 1925 Adams had gained approval for a permanent camp and had that camp set up in time for the second visit of the park commission.

Many old-timers think that the commission was swayed in its final decision by the efforts of Paul Adams at the Mt. Le Conte Camp that August and that the decision to recommend a Great Smoky Mountains National Park was made at the camp.

Final passage of the bill designating the park was eight years away, however, and Mt. Le Conte changed to Le Conte Lodge in those years. During the winter of 1925–26, after the second visit of the park commission, Adams had hand-built the first cabin on the Mt. Le Conte Camp site and shortly thereafter turned the operation of the camp over to Will Ramsey and Jack Huff.

In the following years Huff built more cabins, turning the camp into Le Conte Lodge. Le Conte was retained by the Huffs after the park was formed, and, under the same conditions that prevailed at the Wonderland Club Hotel, they received a lifetime lease in lieu of 50 percent of the appraised value of the lodge.

Again, changes were made in the lease arrangements with the NPS in the 1970s, and the owners of Le Conte Lodge had to agree to several conditions that were imposed on them because of the situation at the lodge.

Sewage had become an apparent problem at the lodge over the years as an increasing number of guests came to Le Conte, and as the lodge tried to accommodate as many as they could. This led to overcrowded conditions that threatened to make the lodge an eyesore to hikers who came to observe a pristine wilderness.

The trails that led to the lodge were also undergoing heavy stress because of the constant pounding they received from horses carrying provisions to the lodge to feed the many guests.

The NPS requirements for a renewed lease were three. One, the lodge had to agree to limit the number of guests to forty a night; two, they had to install chemical toilets instead of using the aging sewer system; and three, they had to agree to bring all their supplies in by helicopter once a year, at which time garbage from the previous season was to be carried out. The lodge owners were willing to abide by these requirements as long as they could continue to operate.

The lodge's popularity has increased, if anything, since these restrictions were made by the NPS, and it fills nightly even though guests have to walk at least five miles to reach it, and those five miles are all over a steep mountain trail. There are four other trails leading to the lodge that aren't as steep, but they are much longer.

[65] The accomodations that await guests when they reach the top don't challenge the Ahwahnee or El Tovar for luxury, either. There are eight small cabins; two larger, dormitory-style cabins; an office with small lobby; and a dining room, all built of logs from the mountains, sitting just below the peak of Mt. Le Conte at 6,500 feet. This makes Le Conte Lodge the highest guest lodge east of the Mississippi River.

None of the cabins have baths; all the running water is located outside, and is cold; and guests have to go down a lane to the chemical toilets. The food in the dining room is often little more

The lobby of the office has the feel of an old mountain cabin.

than reconstituted freeze-dried meals, and can't be called gourmet quality.

What draws so many people to a lodge that offers so little? What it does offer—the finest view in the Smokies and the invigoration of awaking on a chilly morning to hike to Myrtle Point to watch the sun rise.

The solitude of the Smokies is very much a part of the atmosphere at Le Conte Lodge, and modern conveniences such as electricity and telephones are left thousands of feet below. To wake up in the pre-dawn cold of an autumn morning, walk through the mist to reach Myrtle Point, and watch the rising sun light up the multicolored fall forests of the Smokies is something that just can't be found in Gatlinburg or Pigeon Forge. Even a breakfast of dehydrated eggs and canned ham tastes good in the warm dining room as you look out over the valley where the other type of tourist stays—in modern, convenient lodges where you can drive to the door.

[67]

Mt. Rainier National Park

MT RAINIER, THE MOST PHOTOGRAPHED MOUNTAIN IN AMERICA, IS HARD to miss. Its 14,410-foot summit is visible for over 100 miles on a clear day, and it stands as a sentinel over all of western Washington. Its height, glaciers, and inaccessibility drew many early settlers who attempted to climb the peak, and one, James Longmire, discovered a meadow on the western slope of Mt. Rainier in 1883 that was the perfect site for a lodge to house the climbers and explorers who were beginning to flock to the mountain. This meadow was complete with mineral springs where visitors could rest their weary bodies on the way back to civilization after climbing Mt. Rainier or exploring the thick forests of its slopes.

Longmire Springs Hotel and Baths have long since disappeared, but the meadow where they stood is named after Longmire, and today it is the western entrance of the Mt. Rainier National Park.

The Longmire Springs Hotel still stood when Mt. Rainier was declared a national park in 1899, and it was the only lodge near the new park. Guests traveling to the park often spent the night at Longmire before ascending higher up the mountain. Most of those who went farther into the park took the tour offered by the Longmire family to view a meadow located on the southern slope of Mt. Rainier that the Longmires thought was close to what "Heavenly Paradise" must be, and which they named *Paradise Meadows*.

At Paradise Meadows there was a profusion of wildflowers in late July and August that literally burst from the soggy marshes and sloping hillsides. These flowers were subalpine species that survived the long winters covered by a deep snowpack and quickly grew to maturity during the short growing season. The snowpack often lasted well into July, and the flowers were seen sometimes as late as September.

This meadow soon became the favorite site in the park, and the Longmire's tours became even more crowded as the residents of Tacoma and Seattle heard about it.

These crowds also wanted more accommodations near the entrance of the park, and another hotel was built across the road from the Longmire Springs Hotel. This was the National Park Inn.

NATIONAL PARK INN [68]

The Tacoma and Eastern Railroad obtained a permit from the secretary of the interior to build their lodge in 1907, and the building was completed just in time to house visitors who were coming to the park by automobile.

Many of those visitors stayed at the National Park Inn, which could house sixty people in its main building and seventy-five more in tents that were erected next to the inn itself. Increased traffic into the park caused the inn to expand, and in 1911 it was described as being a three-story structure with thirty-six rooms and eighty-six tents. Over 200 guests could be housed when all of these were full.

The demand for rooms near the park grew even more, and in 1917 another hotel building with seventeen rooms was built across the road from the inn where the Longmire Springs Hotel and Baths had stood before it burned.

The Rainier National Park Company bought the franchise and buildings of the National Park Inn from the Tacoma and Eastern in 1918, and soon met with a disaster that was common with early national park inns—their original building burned down. The seventeen-room structure across the road was moved to replace the one that had burned, and it then became known as the National Park Inn Annex, for the main building of the inn had survived the conflagration.

The main building also burned in 1926, and the annex was all that was saved. None of the original buildings of the National Park Inn that were built on the south side of the road to Mt. Rainier in 1907 and 1911 stand today. Instead, the seventeen-room building from the north side of the road is the present National Park Inn.

The kitchen of the present inn was built in 1926 after the rest of the buildings had burned, and it serves guests who stay in the sixteen rooms now rented by the inn. At an age of almost eighty,

This small inn is an unimposing building set at the western entrance of Mt. Rainier National Park.

the inn is one of the oldest continuously-used inns in the state of Washington.

It has continued to thrive, not because of any outstanding attraction to the inn itself, but because of its location. The inn is an unimposing wood structure with few amenities, but it does sit at the western entrance of Mt. Rainier National Park—the busiest entrance to the park.

It also draws a steady clientele of guests who want to stay an extra day near the entrance of the park to visit the Longmire Museum, the oldest national park museum in the country, or who want to walk on the miles of trails that radiate out from Longmire Meadows. The ninety-mile Wonderland Trail that encircles Mt. Rainier begins and ends at Longmire.

The shorter trails lead hikers through solemn forests of Douglas fir, red cedar, and western hemlock, and to secluded meadows. Information about all the trails can be obtained at the Hiker's Information Center located next to the National Park Inn.

Early visitors to the park, as well as today's visitors, weren't satisfied to stay on the lower slopes of Mt. Rainier, and large numbers of them began to camp in the beautiful Paradise Meadows area that was about 3,000 feet farther up the slopes. A road was built into the area in 1911, but only tour buses were allowed over it until 1915, when it was opened to the general public.

Acres of fragile subalpine vegetation were destroyed by the heavy use of the meadow, and the NPS began to worry about how to control the heavy traffic to the area. After a series of delays Stephen Mather, the first director of the National Park Services, told businessmen from Seattle and Tacoma that a new lodge needed to built at Paradise to help control camping in the area, and, though he preferred to have local interests build the inn, he would convince Eastern money to finance the project if they weren't forthcoming with the money. This threat was the impetus needed to get the project started, and construction on the first wing of the new inn began in 1915.

PARADISE INN

The rustic design of the inn is apparent even before you enter the lobby.

Paradise Inn (Washington)

This photo was taken on July 15th. There is even more snow on the ground than this in some years.

A tremendous forest fire had occurred on the western slope of Mt. Rainier in 1885, and huge cedar logs were salvaged from the slopes in 1915 to build the Paradise Inn. These logs were hauled to Paradise Meadows by horses, and were milled on the site. The inn claims to be one of the few large buildings in the world made completely of cedar trees that were taken from a single forest. The Alaska cedar used throughout the original wing can still be viewed in the lobby and in the finish work in both the lobby and dining room.

Almost all of the woodwork done in the lobby was done by one old carpenter during the winter 1915-16. He stayed in the building during the heavy winter and did all the adze work on the hand-hewn cedar logs that are exposed throughout the lobby. He also built many of the furnishings in the lobby, and prime examples of his work are still evident in the large tables, the ornate grandfather clock that stands beside the huge fireplace on the

The exposed log beams, wide windows, and good food all help make the dining room one of the most popular spots at Paradise Inn.

west end of the lobby, and the handmade piano that stands in the lobby.

The carpenter, an old German, obviously didn't have claustrophobia, for the snowfall around Paradise is the heaviest in the world, and the three stories of the inn are frequently completely covered by snow by winter's end. It isn't even unusual to have to go through a tunnel in the snowpack to reach the entrance of the lobby from the parking lot as late as the Fourth of July.

This was true even later in the 1972 season after a world's record snowfall of 1122 inches fell at Paradise in 1971-72. The pack was 305 inches that year and covered all but the very peak of the roof of the Inn. And that year wasn't that unusual for the whole decade of the 1970s. Only the 1976-77 winter had less than 500 inches of snowfall in those ten years, and the average for the decade was 620 inches a year.

While the National Park Inn is open all year, it is easy to see why it would be a mammoth task to keep the Paradise Inn open year-round.

From the time the first wing was finished at the Paradise Inn in 1916 until 1929, there were huge areas of tents surrounding the inn, and the dining room that can handle up to 200 guests at a time drew from the tent campers to fill it.

[73]

Alaskan cedar logs were used throughout the inn.

Both the grandfather clock and the heavy table are examples of the woodwork done by an old German carpenter the winter before the lodge opened.

The inn itself had only thirty-three rooms until 1920, of which only four had baths, but the annex was built that year. The new building contained ninety-two rooms, all with baths to satisfy the more demanding guests who were staying at the inn.

With Mt. Rainier to the north and the Tatoosh Range to the south, the Paradise Inn sits in an unsurpassed surrounding. While the location alone would be enough to draw guests to the inn, there is another attraction at Paradise—mountain climbing. Mt. Rainier is one of the most popular mountain-climbing areas in the country, and its twenty-six glaciers, the most on any one peak in the continental United States, offer outstanding ice-climbing as well.

As many as twenty percent of all guests at the Paradise Inn come these days to at least hike the upper trails of Mt. Rainier, if not to actually climb to the summit. This wasn't always the case. In its early days the Paradise Inn drew a high-class clientele (the DuPonts and Tafts were regulars) that often liked more sedentary activities. Or at least less dangerous ones.

[75] The inn operated their own stables in those years, and guests were welcome to join trail rides guided by the inn, and there were other activities such as bus tours, golf, and bridge to satisfy guests who didn't want to risk going into the primitive, and often dangerous, backcountry.

Bridge was so popular at the inn in the 1930s that the Washington State Bridge Tournament was held on the mezzanine above the lobby each year.

All of these activities are a thing of the past. The ski resort is now closed, there are no longer any stables, and the golf course has been returned to nature. Other than the climbers, who may stay at the inn for a week or more, few guests stay for more than a night today. Tours bring in groups from Seattle and Tacoma, drop the guests off at the inn, and drive them back to the cities the next day.

Most of those short-term guests go away from the inn a little heavier than they come, for the dining room caters to the climbers, and all its meals are ones that can satisfy someone who has just climbed a mountain. While most of the guests aren't going to climb a mountain, it's hard to resist such dining pleasures, and the 200-person dining room is always full.

Olympic National Park

THE OLYMPIC PENINSULA IN WASHINGTON IS A VERY SPECIAL PLACE, and no other spot on the peninsula is more special than Lake Crescent, the largest lake in the Olympic National Park.

President Cleveland established the Olympic Forest Reserve in 1897 to protect the rain forests of the peninsula, and less than ten years later Teddy Roosevelt set aside more of the area as the Mt. Olympus National Monument to protect the large herds of elk that were being decimated for their teeth, popular as watch fobs.

The peninsula was protected more by its isolation than by governmental action in those years, and few roads had been built through its nearly impenetrable forests as late as 1930. To reach the resorts located around Lake Crescent tourists had to travel by ferry boats that criss-crossed the lake.

Only one lodge of the many that were located around the lake before the Olympic National Park was formed is still serving the public, and that is Lake Crescent Lodge.

LAKE CRESCENT LODGE

In 1914 Al Singer built Singer's Lake Crescent Tavern on the east side of Lake Crescent. In those years the only way to reach that side of the lake was by ferry. There were several lodges served by the ferries, and Singer's soon became one of the most popular of all of them.

The guests came to a lodge that had a glassed-in sun porch that gave them a dry and warm place to quietly view the scenery. When the porch got too cool they could go back inside the small lobby where a large stone fireplace drew guests to its warmth.

Today's guests visit the same lodge with the same comforts. Even the dining room off the lobby, with views of both the lake

[77]

The lodge is often enshrouded by fog in the summer.

and the forests, has remained unchanged in the seventy years since Al Singer built his tavern.

Tourists have been able to reach Lake Crescent Lodge by automobile since the first road was built around the eastern side of the lake in 1921-22, but it wasn't until 1931 that the Olympic Loop Highway was opened. This was the first all-weather, paved road around the lake, and the new influx of tourists to the Olympic Peninsula led to a movement to have the entire peninsula designated a national park.

Lake Crescent Lodge played an important role in the final decision to designate much—if not all, as many people wanted—of the peninsula a national park. That decision was made in 1938, after Franklin Roosevelt, along with a party that included senators, representatives, forest service officials, and several famous newspaper men, had visited the Olympic Peninsula in 1937. On that trip the party arrived in Port Angeles, about thirty miles from Lake Crescent, aboard the destroyer *Phelps*, and rode out to Lake Crescent after a parade through downtown Port Angeles.

At Lake Crescent the entire party was housed at the Lake Crescent Lodge while they studied the proposal to make the Olympic Peninsula into a park. As a result of that stay Congress passed the bill establishing the Olympic National Park, and Roosevelt signed it into law in 1938.

The sun porch and five rooms of the main lodge both look out over the lake.

Most of the old resorts around Lake Crescent were bought out by the NPS and closed down. Some remained as privately owned enclaves within the boundaries of the park, however, and continued to operate. Lake Crescent Lodge was one of those bought by the NPS and is the only one of those that still serves the general public. Rosemary Inn still stands next to the Lake Crescent Lodge, but it is used only to house lodge employees and isn't open to the public.

The main building of the Lake Crescent Lodge is the original building of Singer's Lake Crescent Tavern. It remains little changed over the years. No longer are all ten rooms of the lodge rented out, though, for the rooms that face away from the lake are used to house staff members. Only the five rooms that face out over the lake are rented out to the public.

These five offer a prime view of the lake, however, and have lost none of their original ambience, which made the lodge so popular in its early years. And yet, as unlikely as it sounds, these rooms are always among the last to be rented at the lodge and are almost always available on a drop-in basis. Since they share a bath that is down the hall, they aren't popular with today's guests, who are more used to complete accommodations.

Those guests prefer to stay in one of the thirty cottages that surround the main lodge. These were built in the 1920s, and show their age. They are still comfortable, though, and all offer a view of the lake.

Other guests prefer to stay in the more modern motel accommodations that were built at the lodge in the 1950s, and while these rooms are definitely comfortable they have none of the charm of the rest of the lodge.

The Olympic Peninsula offers many recreational opportunities, but guests at the Lake Crescent Lodge who fish have an added benefit. There are two species of trout found in the lake that are found nowhere else. One is the Beardslee trout—often identified

The sun porch is a light and airy spot even when outside is foggy and cold.

The lobby is crowded but guests can still find a place to sit near the old stone fireplace.

as the Beardslee Rainbow—that ranges from eight to twenty pounds, and the other is the Crescenti Cutthroat, which weighs up to ten pounds.

While the lodge has a run-down appearance, particularly the cottages, it is slated for considerable improvements in the next decade by the current concessionaire, and there is even talk of keeping it open year-round instead of just during the summer.

While no one disputes the attractions of the Olympic Peninsula, few people outside the Northwest stay at Lake Crescent Lodge (over 50 percent of the guests come from Seattle), and the lodge's most loyal followers are local landowners who retain title to cabins inside the park boundaries. These people still remember the lodge from its early days and often come to dine today.

They join together to reminisce about the days before the Olympic Loop Highway made it possible for tourists to just drive through the peninsula. In those days visitors stayed long enough to learn about the area and to enjoy the ageless beauty of the forests.

Lake Crescent Lodge (Washington)

Many guests who come to the Lake Crescent Lodge understand that the only way you can get a good feel of the Olympic Peninsula is to stay at least a week. They know that a stay at the only old lodge inside the park is a good way to add to the pleasure of visiting the peninsula.

[81]

Oregon Caves National Monument

NO ONE JUST DROPS BY THE OREGON CAVES. IT'S NOT ON THE WAY TO anywhere unless you just happen to be going from Grants Pass, Oregon, to Crescent City, California. Therefore, most of the tourists who take the eighteen miles of narrow and tortuous Oregon Highway 41 between Cave Junction and the Oregon do so for one reason—to see the caves. Most, but not all, for some go to stay at one of the least known, and least publicized, lodges in the national parks, the Oregon Caves Chateau.

OREGON CAVES CHATEAU

The Oregon Caves were first discovered in 1874, but it wasn't until Joaquin Miller, the Poet of the Sierra, visited them in 1907 that a concerted effort was made to preserve them for the future. During the 1890s there were several attempts to develop the caves as a tourist attraction, but their (really its, for there is only one cave, but the name of Oregon Caves has stuck from the early years) isolation prevented any large group of tourists from reaching the caves.

Miller wrote about them after his visit and named them the Marble Halls of Oregon. The publicity that surrounded his visit gave the needed impetus to federal officials to get the caves declared a national monument. President Taft did that in 1909.

Even though they were a national monument, there was no easy way to reach the caves for the next decade. Until 1922 the only way to get to them was by either walking or riding a horse over at least eight miles of mountain trails. There were two trails to choose from when the decision was finally made to build a road, and neither looked promising. The one from the northeast was not as steep as the one from the west, but it was considera-

[83]

Only the upper three stories are visible on the chateau from entrance level.

bly longer and had so many ups-and-downs that it wasn't practical to build a road over it that cars could drive on.

The problem with the trail from the west was steepness. It was shorter, but it rose 2,300 feet in eight miles from the end of the primitive road that ran from what is now Cave Junction. Engineers decided that the problems associated with the climb could be overcome and selected that route for the new road.

It took almost a year to build the eight miles of road, but it opened to traffic on June 26, 1922. Although certainly not a modern freeway, the road was passable, at least in the summer months. It was only one lane when it opened, with pullouts for those times when two cars met.

To protect the tourists, and to keep the road from being overused, a limit of fifty cars per day was set when the road opened. Even with that limit the number of visitors to the caves jumped from 1,100 in 1921 to 12,000 in 1922. This increase led to the first buildings at the caves. The main building was an A-frame chalet that had accommodations for employees but none for tourists. Tent cabins were available to tourists that were near the A-frame between 1924 and 1934, when better accommodations were completed.

In 1923 a group of Grants Pass businessmen had formed the

The stone fireplace and window-side writing desks offer guests several places to relax in the lobby.

Oregon Caves Company, which ran the concession at the monument. As the number of guests began to outstrip the facilities at the caves, they contracted with Gust Lium, a local architect and contractor, to build a lodge at the caves.

Lium had the Oregon Caves Chateau completed for the 1934 season, and within a decade the company had added seven cabins up the hill from the chateau to handle additional guests.

Registrations continued to be high at the Chateau until the mid-1970s, when it began to have vacancies on a regular basis.

Some blame the gas shortage, while others feel that the modern motels that opened in Cave Junction about that time drew off guests. Regardless of the reason, the Oregon Caves Chateau has never regained its drawing power, and it is one of the few lodges in this book where guests can hope to find a room without reservations. And that is sad, for the chateau is just as worthy in its own way as any of the more famous lodges in the national parks.

Little has changed at the chateau since it was completed in 1934. It still sits on the precipitous hillside where its top three stories are visible above the ground level, while the bottom three floors descend down the canyon where they are hidden from view.

The windows of the lobby, indeed almost all the windows in the lodge, offer outstanding views of forests and canyons. The many chairs and sofas in the lobby give even the casual visitor to the lodge an opportunity to enjoy these vistas, and the large double fireplace in the lobby helps take the chill off the cool evenings that occur even in the summer at the caves.

The exposed peeled-pine beams and pillars of the lobby are part of the original interior, but the pillars in the dining room, which is on the level below the lobby and below ground level, are new. The entire dining area had to be rebuilt in the mid-1970s after a large mudslide left several feet of mud in the kitchen and dining areas. The old wooden floors had to be removed because they were buckled from the damp, and the entire dining room and lounge area was remodeled at that time.

There are three floors of bedrooms at the chateau, and the top floor has changed less than any of the others since the chateau opened fifty years ago. The bedrooms there still have handcarved oak bedsteads, open-beam ceilings, and close-up views of treetops.

On the first floor of the chateau there are several suites with both a sitting room and bedroom for those who need more room.

There are no organized activities at the chateau, for most

guests stay for one night only, but there are plenty of trails in the monument for those who want some exercise. For those who are content to sit and relax there is a trout pond that uses the water from the creek running out of the caves (unfortunately the trout served in the dining room come from Idaho rather than the trout pond), and there is even a grand piano in the lobby that is open to all who can play it.

One other thing about the trout pond and the creek from the caves—the water isn't diverted around the chateau, but runs through the dining room, where transplanted ferns grow on the sides of the cement creekbed.

There isn't much to do at the caves. The tour takes a little less than an hour, and things are quiet around the chateau. There is no television, no entertainment, and there is no public telephone service. This makes the Oregon Caves Chateau ideal for guests who want the amenities of a comfortable lodge—spacious rooms and a good dining room—but who want a real break from the outside world. Go, enjoy, and don't tell your friends about this find, for it might become just as popular as it was in previous decades when you had to have reservations well in advance to get a room.

Unlike The Ahwahnee, the grand piano in the lobby of the chateau is open to whoever wants to play it.

Wonderland Club Hotel, Great Smoky Mountains National Park.

Wawona Hotel, Yosemite National Park (top).
The Awahnee, Yosemite National Park (above and opposite).

Le Conte Lodge, Great Smoky Mountains National Park.

Lake Hotel, Yellowstone National Park (above).
Old Faithful Inn, Yellowstone National Park (right).

Old Faithful Inn, Yellowstone National Park (both pages).

Mammoth Hot Springs Hotel, Yellowstone National Park (above, photo by Matt McMillon). Old Faithful Inn, Yellowstone National Park (left). Wawona Hotel, Yosemite National Park (opposite).

CLARK
COTTAGE

HILLS STUDIO

Wawona Hotel, Yosemite National Park (both pages).

Wonderland Club Hotel, Great Smoky Mountains National Park (above).
Le Conte Lodge, Great Smoky Mountains National Park (opposite).

The Awahnee, Yosemite National Park.

The Awahnee, Yosemite National Park.

The Awahnee, Yosemite National Park.

[87]

Yellowstone National Park

YELLOWSTONE NATIONAL PARK WAS THE FIRST NATIONAL PARK IN THE world when it was approved by Congress in 1872. Conservationists had been instrumental in getting the park approved, but a more powerful force behind the move was the Northern Pacific Railroad. Northern Pacific's interest had nothing to do with conservation, though, for they were strictly concerned with increasing their rail profits.

The Washburn Expedition that explored the Yellowstone region in 1870 was financed by Jay Cooke, an agent for the Northern Pacific, and the most powerful supporter of the park was a Montana judge who was a longtime friend of the Northern Pacific.

Northern Pacific's efforts didn't stop when Yellowstone became a park; they actually increased. They wanted to have a strong say in the selection of concessionaires for the park. Not that they were interested in actually running any of the concessions themselves; they just wanted to make sure that whoever received the concessions would be friendly to them.

Toward that end they got a brother-in-law of a Northern Pacific promoter appointed as the first superintendent of the new park. In his position he blocked any concession development until the Northern Pacific pushed its tracks closer to the park, and he attempted to persuade Congress to allow the railroad to build branch lines into the park itself.

His successor turned out to be less faithful to the powerful railroad, though, and the Northern Pacific had him suspended when he favored a move by the Utah and Northern to extend their lines into the park before the Northern Pacific did so.

Conservationists successfully fought Northern Pacific's efforts to extend a line into the region, but that wasn't the end of the company's involvement in the politics of the park. After General Phil Sheridan helped the conservationists convince the secretary of the interior that no railroads should be extended into the park, the Northern Pacific tried another tack to increase their control over the concessions.

They had individuals indebted to them form the Yellowstone Park Improvement Company, which obtained the rights to build several hotels in the park. While Northern Pacific seemed to have no responsibility for this company, it did in fact control it behind the scenes and tried to get all rights to bring passengers to the new lodges.

The subterfuge was not very successful, as the Yellowstone Park Improvement Company was underfinanced and had to be bailed out by the Northern Pacific. Against their desires, the railroad directors found themselves the sole owner of the Yellowstone Park Association, which replaced the debt-ridden Yellowstone Park Improvement Company in 1886.

Who controlled the transportation and lodging concessions for Yellowstone was of considerable financial importance in the first fifty years of the park's existence. Most visitors to the large park—it has more area then Rhode Island and Delaware combined—came to the park on one of several railroads that had railheads near the park, joined a tour on one of the stages that transported tourists around the park, and stayed at a different hotel each night.

One of the most popular of these tours was a five-day trip that began at the Cinnabar terminus of the Northern Pacific Railroad in Montana. Guests were transported by stage eight miles to the old National Hotel at Mammoth Hot Springs inside the park. They spent the afternoon at the springs and headed out to see the rest of the park the second day. After spending lunch hour at Norris Geyser Basin, the stage continued on to the Lower Geyser Basin, where several hotels stood over the years, the most famous of which was the old Fountain Hotel which opened in 1891. The tourists spent two nights there, since the trip to Upper Geyser Basin was handled as a side trip on the next day after the group reached the Fountain Hotel.

The next night was spent at the Grand Canyon of the Yellowstone. Until a road was constructed from Upper Geyser Basin to Lake Yellowstone, this was the last night spent in the park before returning to Mammoth Hot Springs. In 1892 another night was added to this Grand Tour as the Lake Hotel was opened.

These tours were popular with "dudes" from the East who had the money to spend, and the concessionaires attempted to keep other tourists (known as "sagebrushers" in those days) who weren't planning to use the stages and lodges, but who wanted to travel and camp on their own, out of Yellowstone. They were successful in this for a number of years, and it wasn't until 1915, when the objections of the concessionaires were overridden by the park management, that private automobiles were allowed into the park.

These later tourists did benefit from the tours that had been about the only way to see Yellowstone for its first half-century as a park, however, for roads had been built to most of the more sce-
[89] nic spots, and four major hotels were in operation to spend a
night or a week.

Three of those hotels, Lake, Mammoth Hot Springs, and Old Faithful, are still operating. The fourth was torn down in 1959 after the big Yellowstone earthquake. The concessionaire claimed that it was torn down because of damage from the quake, but others think that it was a financial decision—one that destroyed one of the outstanding lodges in the national parks.

The Canyon Hotel was built in 1910-11 overlooking the Grand Canyon of the Yellowstone and was the second hotel to be built in the park that was designed by architect Robert Reamer. This lodge had 700 rooms and had a perimeter of almost one mile.

Most architects feel that the Canyon Hotel was the best example of Reamer's work and was much more sophisticated in style and technique than the earlier Old Faithful Inn.

Three of the four Yellowstone lodges included in this book were either designed by Reamer or have additions to the original buildings that were designed by him. These are the Lake Hotel, Old Faithful Inn, and the Mammoth Hot Springs Hotel. Only Roosevelt Lodge has no connection with the architect, who began the national park rustic design that influenced so many lodges and hotels in the Northwest.

LAKE HOTEL

The Lake Hotel is the oldest of the hotels remaining in Yellowstone, and construction on it was begun in 1889. Construction was slow, though, and the west wing didn't open until 1891. The wing had only eighty rooms, and no more were added until 1903, when the number of rooms was doubled.

More additions in 1904 increased the number of rooms to 210, and the rather plain building was changed to a colonial-style

The porticoes and sitting room were added in 1904 to give the hotel its colonial façade.

structure as the existing gables on the lake side of the building were extended and large pillars were added to them to make the porticoes that now dominate the west wing.

Further remodeling was done between 1919 and 1923. In those years the porte-cochere was added over the hotel driveway, and the east wing, with 113 rooms and fifty-nine baths, was completed. These later additions were designed by Reamer.

By 1923 what had begun as a plain, small hotel had been expanded to its present size and extended 300 feet along the shore of Yellowstone Lake in colonial splendor. Today its soft yellow, set off by the stark white trim, stands out among the green of pines that have grown almost to the top of the hotel's four stories in the past half-century.

Earlier years are often seen as a time when tourists were more relaxed and when people spent enough time in one spot to rest before they moved on. This view isn't necessarily correct, for the Grand Tour of Yellowstone that covered most of the major regions of the park in a five- or six-day period were far from relaxing. In fact, they were downright hectic.

In a guide to Yellowstone that was written in 1923 Reau Campbell said, "The Lake Hotel that was once called the 'Colonial' is a fine place to stay awhile even if you didn't do anything but watch the people come in the afternoon and go away in the morning, a different crowd every day, and yet always the same, always in a hurry, never stopping to rest or to see anything."

Sounds a lot like today when tour buses pull into the Lake Hotel, disgorge their loads, and pull out to pick up another load headed for another hotel. But the Lake Hotel is still a quiet and

This stone water fountain is only one of the many small extras that Robert Reamer added to the interior of the hotel.

The exterior renovation hadn't been completed when this photo was taken in 1982, as can be seen along the bottom of the wall.

serene lodge for those who want to do nothing but relax. The tile-mantled fireplace in the lobby still warms guests on cool evenings, and the low-ceilinged sitting room that juts out from the

The low-ceilinged sitting room is a comfortable open area with an excellent view of the lake.

lake-side of the hotel is still filled with caned chairs and sofas well-worn to the human form.

Extensive restoration has been done on the hotel in the past several years, and the old building that is reputed to be the second oldest, and second largest, wood hotel in the country (only the Mackinac Island Hotel is supposedly older and larger) is once again welcoming guests to a colonial atmosphere in a serene setting on the shore of Yellowstone Lake. Not that it hasn't been open, for it has only closed three times in its history. One time was in 1918–19 for World War I; another was from 1933 to 1937 because of the Depression; and the last was from 1940 to 1946 because of World War II.

It's just that the atmosphere became one of a run-down hotel for a period in the 1960s and 1970s. The previous concessionaire in Yellowstone did little to maintain its hotels, and the Lake Hotel became a faded yellow building with a decrepit appearance that was far from welcoming. That has changed with the renovation, and there are plans to extend the hotel's season into the winter to handle the increasing demand for winter trips to Yellowstone.

Two of the other lodges already extended their seasons, and that is an indication of the popularity of the old hotels of Yellowstone. The most popular of those is undoubtedly the first lodge built by Robert Reamer in the park, the Old Faithful Inn.

The porte-cochere was added in 1919 and is seldom used today as most tour buses deposit their passengers in the rear of the hotel.

OLD FAITHFUL INN

Until 1904 tourists who wanted to see Old Faithful Geyser either had to make a rough ten-mile trip from the Fountain Hotel or spend the night in one of a succession of disreputable lodges that were erected near the geyser over the years.

The more affluent tourists who visited the park began to put pressure on the Yellowstone Park Association, which was a subsidiary of the Northern Pacific Railroad, to build a first-class hotel near the geyser. The Northern Pacific had found that building hotels was a money-losing proposition in Yellowstone, not a money-making one, and wanted to avoid any more investments in them. With time, however, a change in the National Park Service policy helped convince the company that a new hotel might be a profitable investment.

Until 1900 the NPS had a policy that no building was to be built any closer than one-quarter mile to any natural object of interest, but they were convinced by concessionaires that this regulation was too stiff and changed it to one-eighth of a mile in 1901.

This change, plus an increase in competition for tourists dollars from local interests, caused Northern Pacific to reconsider its position. In 1902 Harry Childs, the president of the Yellowstone
[95] Park Association, hired a young, inexperienced architect, twenty-nine-year old Robert Reamer, to design a lodge for the Old Faithful area.

In a time when most hotels were built to be monuments themselves, and to stand out from their surroundings, Reamer decided to do something different at Old Faithful. He decided to use native materials that would fit in with the surroundings, and thus began the national-park-rustic period of architecture that was to last in the West for almost half a century.

Construction of the inn began in late summer 1903 and continued through the winter. Rhyolite, an igneous rock from an earlier time when the Yellowstone area was dominated by volcanoes, was quarried nearby, and tons—500 tons for the immense fireplace alone—were skidded over the snow to the construction site. On top of the stone foundation, straight lodge pole pines were laid down to form the lower walls of what has been called the largest log building in the world.

The tall center structure of the inn rises 85 feet and stands looking over the Upper Geyser Basin at Yellowstone.

The porte-cochere that juts out from the front of the inn is situated so that disembarking passengers see Old Faithful Geyser.

Inside, the straight beams were supported by hundreds of twisted limbs and trunks of deformed lodge pole pines to give the eighty-five-foot-high lobby a rustic appearance that had never before been attempted in a large first-class inn.

The first part of the inn was completed in time for the 1904 season, and the public's reception of it was best expressed by Charles Adams of the famous New England family. "Old Faithful Inn," he wrote. "Try to imagine an immense structure . . . with wings and nooks, and a broad veranda giving nice, quiet little secluded spots . . . the big double doors with hand made, wrought iron knocker, hinges and bolts, leading into an inside court, covered only be the roof . . . the stairway leading by turns up to the top, and promenades on the different floors looking down into the court all made from logs, many twisted into appropriate and fantastic shapes for the particular spot by their natural growth from the knotted forest in the Park. . . . All I can say is that the greatest travelers in the world say, 'There is nothing in the world like it or to compare with Old Faithful Inn.' "

There still isn't. Little has been changed on the main building that Reamer designed in 1902, although two wings have been added to it—the east one in 1913 and the west one in 1927. Neither of these has the total rustic feeling of the original inn, how-

This iron work can be seen on the inside of the front door of the lobby.

ever, for "motel modern" had begun to creep into the rustic lodges of the park by the 1920s, and the rooms in the west wing are little different from what you find in motels today.

That is in stark contrast to the rooms in the original inn. Even today they are sparse, have exposed light bulbs hanging from the ceiling, and have rough-sawn board walls. Also, few have baths, since that was a real luxury in the early 1900s.

Like the rooms, the inn retains the rustic atmosphere created by Reamer. The first-floor lobby has been rearranged several times over the years, but from the second floor on up there have been no major structural changes made at all.

The fireplace that dominates the lobby is fourteen feet square at the base, has eight fireplaces (only two still work after the 1959 earthquake), and has a twenty-foot-long wrought-iron clock on the side facing the front entrance of the lobby.

Little about the inn is predictable. For example, the lobby and rooms don't face the famous natural feature that attracts millions of people each year, the Old Faithful Geyser. Instead, the building was designed so that guests could see it when they alighted from their coaches under the porte-cochere in front of the hotel, and the roof of the porte-cochere is the most popular observation site for inn guests to see Old Faithful spout.

Another popular observation site for years was the thirteen foot by seventy-two foot observation platform on top of the eighty-five-foot-high lobby. Unfortunately, both this platform and the upper balconies (including the famous crow's nest or tree house near the top) have been closed to guests, since the 1959 earthquake caused structural damage on some of the supporting beams.

The lower three balconies are still open to guests, though, and from them you can get a bird's-eye view of the sixty-four-foot-square lobby, and of the many twisted supports that hold up the beams of the inn. Much of the original ironwork of the inn can also be seen from the balconies. The wrought-iron clock, the massive fireplace tools, including a huge popcorn popper, and the many lamps on pillars throughout the lobby were all forged on the site by an old blacksmith by the name of Colpitts. He also did the ironwork that can be seen on the split-log double doors that lead into the lobby both from the front and rear.

The ironwork on the front door, with locking bar, heavy hinges, handmade lock and key, and coiled spring bell is by far the most spectacular example of Colpitts's work.

All of the logs in the lobby were left unpeeled when they were erected in 1904, but all the bark was removed in 1940 because too many guests were complaining that they were snagging their suits—yes, suits, for guests in those days wore their finest, no jeans for them—and the housekeepers were complaining about how hard it was to dust them.

While the removal of the bark changed the appearance of the logs, it also exposed the fine network of tunnels that bark beetles had dug under the bark before the trees were cut. The logs were varnished in 1960, and today they have deepened to a dark sheen which reflects the light from the many small light fixtures that hang from the pillars.

Several years ago the National Park Service and TWA Services, Inc., began a restoration of the inn, which had deteriorated badly over the years. This restoration was supervised by a historical architect from the NPS, and an effort was made to replace all shingles, beams, and other items in a manner identical to the original mode of construction. This involved hours of looking through a

The rafters are a forest of straight and twisted lodge pole pine.

magnifying glass at old photos of the exterior of the inn to determine how Reamer had designed it.

This wasn't easy, for Reamer didn't do things the easy way. Shingles were placed differently on different parts of the outside walls, and few of the windows of the inn have the same design in their window panes. Some have square panes, some have snowflake designs, while others have diamond shapes. This made restoration difficult, but the architect who supervised the work, Andy Beck, was so conscientious that even the ends of the log beams that were replaced with epoxy were made to duplicate the beveled ends of the original logs, and the bevels were even slanted the same way if that could be determined from photos.

Even trained observers miss some things, though, and Andy Beck is no exception. He had spent hours poring over old photos and papers of the inn and thought that he knew just about all there was to know about its history. That was until a guest came up to him one day and said, "Where are the old panels that used to hang in the Bear Pit?" Beck knew that the Bear Pit was the old lounge (it's now a snack bar), but he didn't know anything about any panels. The guest went on to say that when he had visited the inn with this family in 1940 there had been a group of wooden panels on the walls of the lounge that depicted bears in human-type activities. Beck began to search for these panels, found that there had once been twelve of them, and finally discovered nine in a private home in Montana.

Six of those nine were back up on the walls of the original Bear Pit by 1982, and the others were being restored so they could also be exhibited.

Many things have changed around the Old Faithful Inn since it was built, even if the building itself hasn't changed that much. A large searchlight used to stand atop the observation platform above Old Faithful Inn, and it was turned on Old Faithful Geyser every night so the affluent guests at the inn could see all the eruptions. Occasionally the man who operated the light would turn it on some bear or elk that happened to come near the inn, and that practice gave Charles Adams an idea on one of his visits to Old Faithful.

Adams loved the inn but abhorred its clientele. He thought they were a slothful bunch of rich snobs, and he often wished to join the tourists at the nearby tent camps where there always seemed to be more fun and activity than at the inn. Adams wanted to have some fun, and he thought he knew how to have it.

Younger guests at the inn were known to have as much fun with members of the opposite sex as the guests at the tent cabins, and couples who went out into the woods to spend a quiet evening together were known as "rotten loggers." One evening Charles Adams decided to have some fun with these couples. He talked the man who operated the searchlight into letting him use it, and he began to scan the forests around the inn. He soon spotted some rotten loggers who were quite surprised to be in the spotlight. Adams held the light on them until he could recognize who they were, and until they ran for cover. He enjoyed his prank as he told it to other guests, but understandably the younger set wasn't overjoyed with his idea of a good time.

The tent cabins are gone, the spotlight no longer shines at night, and guests are forbidden to climb to the observation platform, but a stay at the Old Faithful Inn is still an enjoyable stay at the first of the "rustic" lodges in our national parks.

Both Lake Hotel and Old Faithful Inn were filled to overflowing in the busy decade of the 1920s, and large lodges with groups of cabins were constructed next to both during the middle of the decade. These were called Lake Lodge and Old Faithful Lodge, and the main buildings housed restaurants. showers, shops, and sitting rooms, while guests stayed in individual cabins that offered cover from the elements, but none of the luxury of the hotels.

There was one lodge built in the park, though, that was the forerunner of the latter two that wasn't built as an adjunct to a more luxurious hotel. That was Roosevelt Lodge.

[101]

ROOSEVELT LODGE

Roosevelt Lodge sits away from any of the major scenic areas of Yellowstone. There are no falls, no rivers, no hot springs, and no geysers nearby to attract tourists, and the area was avoided by most of the early Grand Tours. It wasn't until Teddy Roosevelt visited the area in 1903 with naturalist John Burroughs that the vast northeastern corner of the park became well known.

This corner of the park is made up of rolling hills, sage-covered flatlands, and an occasional river that flows out of the pine for-

The long, low main lodge houses the registration desk, restaurant, and sitting room. Square dances are often held there. Much is made of Roosevelt's supposed visits to the area, but there is no indication that he ever camped where the lodge sits.

The interior of the main lodge is very rustic and informal.

ests that cover some of the higher hills. While there are no big natural sites to see, outdoor activities such as horseback riding, fishing, trail trips, and a petrified forest to visit all have continued to draw guests to the lodge since it was built in 1906 to commemorate Roosevelt's visit to the area and to capitalize on his popularity.

A large central lodge building with restaurant, shop, fireplace, and laundry facilities sits on the edge of a forest, and eighty-eight cabins radiate out from the lodge to house guests who come for at least a week at a time to enjoy the Western atmosphere that is complete with stagecoach rides, Western-style cookouts, and square dances.

The popularity of this lodge led to the construction of the lodges and cabins at Lake, Old Faithful, and Mammoth Hot Springs. The latter is the site of the last of the old hotels and lodges to be built in Yellowstone, the Mammoth Hot Springs Hotel and Cabins.

The cabins at Roosevelt Lodge sit in groves of pine and look out over sage-covered hills beyond.

[103]

MAMMOTH HOT SPRINGS HOTEL AND CABINS

The first Mammoth Hotel was built in 1883 to house the tourists who disembarked from the Northern Pacific at either Cinnabar or Livingston, Montana. The hot springs at Mammoth were the first stop on the grand tour from the north, and were often the last stop on the way out of the park.

There was construction on the hotel for a number of years as it was expanded to accommodate the increasing number of guests, until, by 1936, the area was a hodge-podge of ill-fitting buildings

The modernistic buildings of this hotel stand in stark contrast to the rustic designs of most other national park lodges.

[104]

The hotel and cabins together form a small village that is very busy during the summer season.

Contrasting stark white walls and natural wood floors exaggerate the modern design of Reamer.

that housed everything from the hotel to a general store. Not only was the area unplanned, many of the buildings were unsafe.

In 1936 most of the old hotel was razed—only the large east wing was saved—and Robert Reamer was hired to design a new hotel. This hotel barely fits with the criterion set down for the book (lodges and hotels that are at least fifty years old). In fact, it

The dining room is formal rather than rustic.

doesn't meet them, for the hotel was only forty-five years old when the research for the book was completed.

It was included, however, for two reasons: (1) it was the last major project in Yellowstone designed by Robert Reamer, and (2) it is one of the only examples of the transition from "national park rustic" architecture to "motel modern" architecture left in the national parks. Most of the lodges and hotels in the parks were either built before World War II and are rustic in design, or were built in the 1950s and are modern in design.

The Mammoth Hot Springs Hotel and Cabins is neither. It best fits into what has been called Reamer's Art Deco period, and its stark white interiors are set off by dark wood paneling, and fixtures are definitely more arty than those in any of the other lodges covered in this book.

The porte-cochere is square, flat-roofed, and has square columns supporting it. The lobby has large picture windows, a modernistic fireplace in the center, and paneled walls.

Even the Map Room is more functional than rustic. It has a large map of the United States on the north wall made of over a dozen different types of hardwood, and it is more of an auditorium that seats as many as 200 people than it is a sitting room.

The Mammoth Hot Springs Hotel was definitely designed for the modern tourist, and even its restaurant, which is housed in a separate building from the hotel, has a much more urban appearance than a national park atmosphere.

The hotel is now used as a stopping-off spot, not as a final destination as the Lake Hotel and Old Faithful Inn often are, and it offers a hectic air that is probably not unlike that offered by the old Mammoth Hotel in the late 1800s when it was the first stop in the new Yellowstone National Park for tour after tour.

Yosemite National Park

YOSEMITE IS ONE PARK WHERE THE RAILROADS HAD LITTLE TO DO WITH either the designation of the park or the construction of any of the hotels and lodges there. Roads have been more important to Yosemite, for the park was located much nearer large populations centers from the time it was approved in 1890.

A number of hotels and lodges have been built in Yosemite in the past century, but most have either been torn down because they became outdated, or have burned to the ground. The last of those was the Glacier Point Lodge, which burned in the late 1950s.

There are two major hotels left in the park. One, the Wawona Hotel, has been in continuous operation since 1879, eleven years before the park was established. This makes it the oldest lodge included in this book. The other hotel in Yosemite is The Ahwahnee, a hotel that is synonomous with luxury.

The Ahwahnee sits in the middle of the Yosemite Valley, near the scenic sites that are most often associated with the park. The Wawona is located twenty-seven miles south of the valley in an area that is more often associated with Sequoia National Park than with Yosemite, but the southern part of Yosemite National Park has some of the largest Big Trees found in California, and that was where the Wawona Hotel was built in 1879.

WAWONA HOTEL

In 1911 a visitor to the Wawona Hotel wrote, "Inertia creeps into your system . . . You are ever ready to drop into a chair and listen to the wind sighing through the trees and river singing its never-ending song."

Each of the six buildings of the Wawona are named from history of the lodge.

In those years the hotel was a self-sufficient enclave miles from the nearest settlement. Telephones had reached the small village in 1905 and electricity in 1908, but it was still far from the Central Valley towns of Fresno and Merced. Far, but accessible by stage coach that ran along what is now State Highway 41. Over this road visitors came to view the wonders of Yosemite Valley, and Wawona was a good stopping point.

So many visitors stopped by the Wawona that by the 1920s, the peak years for the hotel, there were over twenty Chinese working in the kitchen, garden, and laundry to serve the many guests. The food served in the kitchen in those days came from their own gardens, their own dairy, and from the woods and streams that were nearby.

Fresh trout and venison were common meals, and one young employee of the hotel is said to have caught over 32,000 trout in two seasons to feed the guests.

In the growth years before the Wawona became part of the

This banister is an example of the fine craftsmanship that went into the construction of the hotel.

Yosemite Park and Curry Company, it grew from one building to eight and increased the size of its grounds to almost 4,000 acres. On these there were a swimming pool, golf course, three fountains, a lake, and an airport. Most of these features are gone now, although there are tennis courts, a golf course, and one fountain left from the earlier years.

There is nothing outstanding about the buildings that compose the hotel, but they do have a charm and an elegance that is more often found at a Western resort than at a national park hotel. All

Dining is a pleasurable experience in the open dining room that looks out over the open space in front of the hotel.

the hotel buildings have names, and one of them, the Pavilion, was Thomas Hill's studio. Hill was a famous landscape painter who helped advertise the natural beauties of Yosemite in the late 1800s and early 1900s.

Many of the buildings at the Wawona Hotel have been restored to their original style, and nearby the Pioneer Yosemite History Center offers hotel guests a look at what life was like in the Wawona area around the time the Wawona Hotel opened in 1879.

The other hotel in Yosemite is at the far end of the spectrum from the Wawona Hotel. It was built relatively late, in 1927, and is an example of a luxury hotel that was built for the wealthy.

The small sitting room off the main lobby is reminiscent of the relaxed and opulent early years of the Wawona.

This is one of six buildings where guests stay at the hotel.

Even the small details in the woodwork were carefully crafted.

THE AHWAHNEE

The *The* is always capitalized, and *Hotel* is never added. It's The Ahwhanee, and that's the way it was meant to be. From the time this six-story building was in its planning stages, it had an aura of exclusivity that was without precedence in the national parks, which were developed so that all citizens of our nation could enjoy the natural wonders that had been set aside as parks and monuments as inexpensively as possible.

Even though this had been the philosophy of the National Park Service under the direction of Stephen Mather, its first director, there was never any doubt about the type of clientele Mather hoped to draw to The Ahwahnee. A press release sent out as it opened said, "The Ahwahnee is designed quite frankly for people who know the delights of luxurious living, and to whom the artistic and material comforts of their environment are important."

It was unusual for Mather to so blatantly promote a hotel for the wealthy inside one of the national parks, but he did. And all because Lady Astor had refused to spend the night in Yosemite,

Mather's favorite park. She had claimed that all the hotels there were too primitive for her tastes. Mather was chagrined about the incident and vowed that Yosemite would have a first-class hotel that offered VIP service to satisfy the most critical of the famous and the near famous.

He got that hotel by forcing a merger of the two private concessionaires then operating in Yosemite and including a clause in their contract that called for the construction of a new, fireproof hotel in the valley.

This new hotel was to become the Ahwahnee, and the Yosemite Park and Curry Company was glad to have the opportunity to build it. A new year-round highway to Yosemite had opened in 1925, and wealthy tourists were coming to Yosemite in even larger numbers. The Ahwahnee would be an opportunity for the new concessionaires to greatly benefit from this influx.

They wanted to get the hotel built as quickly as possible, so they found an architect, approved his plans, and hired a San Francisco-based contractor—all within six months. The contractor promised the company that he would have The Ahwahnee completed in time for a late-1926 opening, and at a cost of about $600,000. Then, as now, contractors' promises were often meaningless. The Ahwahnee wasn't completed until almost seven months after the contract deadline, and its costs had risen to over $1 million by completion.

Not all of the delays or cost overruns were the contractor's fault, for the original plans for the hotel were so elaborate that it would have been almost impossible to have built such a structure, and even if it had been possible, the costs would have been prohibitive.

The Ahwahnee in its completed state was much less elaborate than what had been planned, but that is not to say that it wasn't extravagant. The interior decoration alone added another $250,000—more than the total costs of most of the lodges in this book—to the cost of the hotel. And the results were spectacular. They remain so to this day, and it is hard to imagine that the building, setting, and interior didn't match the dreams of the people involved in 1926–27.

The dining hall at The Ahwahnee today seats 350 diners in a room that is 130 feet long, fifty-one feet wide, and thirty-four feet high. The walls have huge stone columns separtating the many windows, and the ceiling beams, plus the ten log columns supporting them, are all barked sugar pine trees that have slowly darkened with age.

Along the south wall of the hall are ten high windows that give diners a view of Glacier Point, and the spray of Yosemite Falls can be seen through the mammoth alcove windows at the west end of the room.

As large and fine as this dining hall is, it holds only a third as many diners as the original plans called for, and much of the rest of the hotel was scaled down accordingly.

Both the setting and the interior of the dining room are great, but the food served there at least matches, if not surpasses, both. No longer is the kitchen so crowded with specialty cooks that the cost for preparing meals is outrageous, as it was in the early years of The Ahwahnee, but the chefs there rate among the finest in the country.

Not only is the food excellent and the setting unsurpassed, but tradition still reigns at The Ahwahnee. It may be located in a vacation spot, and its standards may have dropped some in the past fifty years, but the management at The Ahwahnee still requires that men wear a coat (a tie is suggested) to dinner and that women be appropriately dressed.

There are thirteen other public rooms on the ground floor and mezzanine. Of these the most impressive is the Great Lounge. This seventy-seven foot-long, fifty-one-foot-wide, and twenty-four-foot-high room is a classic example of the quiet gentility of the period in which The Ahwahnee was built. It has huge fireplaces, kept full of fire on chilly days and evenings, and an abundance of overstuffed chairs and sofas where guests can enjoy their stays in solitude and tranquility if they desire.

The Great Lounge also contains some of the finest examples of the Indian motif that is central to the interior decoration theme of the hotel. The husband-and-wife team of Drs. Phyllis Ackerman and Arthur Pope developed this theme in 1926, and it is still dominant all through the hotel from the Indian design on the lobby floor to the narrow borders around the top of the bedroom walls.

The most striking feature of the Great Lounge is the group of ten floor-to-ceiling windows that are topped with five-by-six-foot stained glass panels that are Indian basket designs. These panels were the creation of Jeanette Dyer Spender, who studied at the Louvre before coming to Yosemite. Her design work on the panels so impressed the Yosemite Park and Curry Company management that they hired her as the permanent interior decorator of The Ahwahnee. She stayed in that position until 1972, and more than anyone else preserved the continuity of the original motif in

The high, open-beamed ceiling of the dining hall gives the large room a feeling of openness.

the interior of The Ahwahnee.

The Ahwahnee opened on July 14, 1927, with ninety-seven private rooms, each with its own bath, and all complete with pewter inkstands and ashtrays, along with handloomed bedspreads and blankets. Many of the original furnishings are gone, and to a most unlikely spot. Fifty special guests had been invited to spend the night at The Ahwahnee after opening day, before the general public was allowed to register. These guests were all wealthy and famous, but they took inkstands, ashtrays, bedspreads, and blankets as "momentoes" of the occasion. They even took some of the

The Great Lounge always offers a quiet refuge for guests at The Ahwanee.

prized Indian baskets that had been on display on the mezzanine.

These fifty guests had been served by a staff that included elevator attendants, shoeshine boys, over fifty waiters and waitresses, plus a kitchen crew top-heavy with specialty chefs. All this staff, plus the normal complement of housekeeping staff, wasn't able to stop the thefts, and security was tightened considerably before the general public began registering the next day.

This group of fifty special guests was followed by many others who fit the image of those Mather had envisioned as frequenting The Ahwahnee. Less than two weeks after it opened The Ahwahnee had its first famous, as opposed to just wealthy, guest. Herbert Hoover, then secretary of commerce, checked in on July 26, 1927. Although Hoover returned to The Ahwahnee many times over the years he almost checked out in a fit of anger this first visit.

It is said he went fishing in the nearby Merced River, as he was to do many times as he revisited The Ahwahnee, and was refused admittance to the hotel lobby when he returned in his dirty and fishy smelly clothes. The doorman on duty adamantly refused to believe that a guest of The Ahwahnee would dress in such a manner, and it was only after much difficulty that Hoover was able to convince him otherwise. This incident enraged Hoover, but after a long talk with the manager he finally agreed to finish out his stay.

[119] Other famous and near-famous guests followed Hoover, and before the Depression The Ahwahnee was more like a private club than a public hotel in a national park. The guest list was selective, and the "common tourist," if not kept out, was at least actively discouraged from staying there.

These early years were the beginning of many traditions at The

The solarium off the Great Lounge is a good place to read or play games when the weather is bad outside.

Ahwahnee, some of which have disappeared over the years, but others have increased in popularity and are stronger today then ever. One of these is the Bracebridge Dinner, which is held in the dining hall each Christmas and New Year's Day.

The first of this tradition was held on Christmas Day 1927, when members of the management of the Yosemite Park and Curry Company, along with some interested guests, put on a pageant that was a reenactment of Washington Irving's 1819 tale of Christmas at Bracebridge Hall in Yorkshire. In that tale Squire Bracebridge entertains his family and friends in a pageant where food, drink, music, and drama are all combined to make a gala event.

All of those in attendance at Bracebridge Hall enjoyed the event, and anyone lucky enough to get reservations for this annual spectacle is sure to enjoy the event as much as Irving's characters did. The Bracebridge Dinner is held in the dining hall, and there just isn't enough room to accommodate all the guests who would like to attend. A lottery has been set up where all guests who would like to attend send in their names about a year before they want to come, and names are drawn so the lucky ones can go.

This has been the strongest tradition at The Ahwahnee, and the only times that it has not been performed were the three years during World War II when the Navy commandeered The Ahwahnee as a convalescent hospital to rehabilitate sick and injured men. During those years The Ahwahnee was closed to the public, and the Great Lounge was converted into a dormitory for 350 men. The mezzanine bar became a Catholic chapel during that period.

The Navy returned the operation of The Ahwahnee to the Yosemite Park and Curry Company in 1946, and the first public event held after it was refurbished was the Bracebridge Dinner on Christmas Day 1946.

The Bracebridge was one tradition that made it through the trying years of the Depression and World War II, but many others at The Ahwahnee broke down during that period. Business was so bad during the 1930s that The Ahwahnee began advertising for guests, and the only thing that kept it from closing its doors was the rent paid by a group of prominent San Francisco Bay Area families who used the seven small cottages that had been built next to the main lodge during the busy 1920s as summer cabins.

To help their advertising campaign The Ahwahnee hired a

young, unknown photographer to make still and motion pictures of The Ahwahnee and Yosemite Valley that could be used for promotional purposes. There is no record of how successful the campaign was, but the photographer's name, Ansel Adams, has become synonymous with Yosemite Valley.

Adams became very much a part of the in-group at The Ahwahnee, and became active in the Bracebridge Dinner production. He rewrote the script, played the piano and acted in the event for many years.

[121] The exclusivity of The Ahwahnee began to disappear during the Depression and was all but gone by the end of the war. The famous continued to flock to Yosemite to enjoy The Ahwahnee's luxuries, but they found that it was no longer a private club for them only. Anyone was welcome. They also discovered, however, that the management still attempted to maintain a atmosphere of tranquility at the hotel.

This wasn't always easy, and it wasn't necessarily the "new guests" who caused the problems. One example was an incident that involved the Steinway grand piano that sits in the Great Lounge. There was, and is, a rule that guest must obtain permission from the manager to play the piano. One January night in 1947 the manager heard the piano being played without his permission and stalked into the lounge to stop the playing.

Stop it he did, and without regard to what guests were involved. As far as he was concerned all guests had to obey the rules, regardless of their reputation. It didn't matter to him that it was Desi Arnez playing the piano, and that Judy Garland was singing along. There were the other guests to be considered.

This incident caused a furor among the Hollywood crowd that had been frequenting The Ahwahnee, and many of them boycotted the hotel for several years afterwards.

After fifty years of operation, The Ahwahnee still maintains an atmosphere that hangs heavy with the feelings of opulence and exclusivity that was its trademark from the beginning. This feeling can't be found in many of the lodges in this book, but it is only a feeling now. All people are invited to stay at The Ahwahnee, if they can afford the rates.

All guests are still expected to maintain a quiet demeanor inside the hotel, though, and to present themselves in a dignified and respectable manner appropriate to the setting. This means they must dress for meals and behave quietly in all public rooms.

The atmosphere, decoration, and quality of service haven't changed much at The Ahwahnee over the years, but one impor-

The basket design over the fireplace outside the Great Lounge was drawn before The Ahwahnee opened.

tant change was made in 1969. Until then The Ahwahnee operated on the American Plan, which included three full and elaborate meals in the cost of the rooms. As the clientele of the hotel changed over the years, from one that was generally sedentary and came to The Ahwahnee to rest, relax, and not venture out for strenuous activities to one that comes not only to enjoy the luxury of The Ahwahnee, but also to participate in skiing, hiking, and mountain climbing, the hotel found that fewer and fewer guests were available for all three meals.

They then changed to the European Plan, and guests can now choose which of their meals they want to eat at The Ahwahnee. Active guests also have the option of having gourmet sack lunches prepared for them by the kitchen to enjoy on outings.

Tourist Information

CRATER LAKE NATIONAL PARK

Crater Lake Lodge
Crater Lake National Park
Crater Lake, Oregon 97604
(503) 594-2511

Season—Mid-June to mid-September
Rates—Hotel, $25.00 to $66.00
Cottages, $18.00 to $30.00
Reservations—Six months for a lakeview room. One month for others.
Comments—The seventy-eight lodge rooms vary from double bed with sink only to suites with queen bed and bath with lake view.

DEATH VALLEY NATIONAL MONUMENT

Furnace Creek Inn
Fred Harvey Company
Death Valley, California 92328
(800) 622-0838 for California residents
(800) 227-4700 for all others

Season—Mid-October to first of May
Rates—$155.00 per person double occupancy for modified American plan (breakfast and dinner)
Reservations—One year in advance for major holiday periods and between January and May. Six to nine months for October to December.
Comments—All sixty-eight rooms and one suite offer outstanding accommodations, but the best rooms are those with a west view over the valley.

Glacier Park Lodge
Glacier Park, Inc.
East Glacier, Montana 59434
(406) 226-4841
Season—Mid-May to end of September
Rates—Standard rooms (104), $38.00 to $46.00
Tourist rooms (49), $33.00 to $41.00
Suites (2), $69.00
Reservations—Two to three months in advance.
Comments—The only difference between the tourist and standard rooms is that the standard are in the annex, which is a little quieter than the main lodge. The $5.00 extra isn't worth it unless you are a very light sleeper.

Lake McDonald Lodge
Glacier Park, Inc.
East Glacier, Montana 59434
(406) 226-4841
Season—Mid-May to end of September
Rates—Standard rooms (28), $38.00 to $46.00
Reservations—Two to three months in advance.
Comments—There area also cabins and motel rooms available at the lodge for those who want to be away from the main lodge.

Many Glacier Hotel
Glacier Park, Inc.
East Glacier, Montana 59434
(406) 226-4841
Season—Mid-May to end of September
Rates—Standard rooms (68), $38.00 to $46.00
Tourist rooms (129), $33.00 to $41.00
Suites and family rooms (8), $69.00
Reservations—Two to three months in advance. More if you want to be sure to get a room with a view of the lake.

Prince-of-Wales Hotel
Glacier Park, Inc.
East Glacier, Montana 59434
(406) 226-4841
Season—Mid-May to end of September
Rates—Standard rooms (66), $45.00 to $55.50
Tourist rooms (20), $38.00 to $48.00
Suite, $82.50
Reservations—Two to three months in advance. More if you

want a lake-side view.

Comments—The only difference between standard and tourist is that the tourist rooms are on the fifth floor, and there is elevator service only to the fourth floor.

The reservation address and phone given above is open only from mid-May to end of season. The address and phone for September 30 to May 15 is—

Glacier Park, Inc.
Suite 7
1735 E. Ft. Lowell Road
Tucson, Arizona 85719
(602) 795-0377

GRAND CANYON NATIONAL PARK

El Tovar

Grand Canyon National Park Lodges
P.O. Box 699
South Rim
Grand Canyon, Arizona 86023
(602) 638-2401

Season—Year-round

Rates—Standard double (36), $60.00
Standard queen (14), $63.00
Deluxe King (15), $65.00
Suites (12), $95.00 to $110.00

Reservations—Four months for all rooms except suites. At least nine months for suites, and a year for view suites.

Comments—Try to get one of the view suites if you want to enjoy the canyon at all times of the day in complete solitude.

Bright Angel Lodge

Grand Canyon National Park Lodges
P.O. Box 699
South Rim
Grand Canyon, Arizona 86023
(602) 638-2401

Season—Year-Round

Rates—Standard rooms (6), $27.00 to $30.00
Rim cabins w/o fireplace (8), $45.00
Rim cabins with fireplace (4), $50.00
Dormitory-style rooms (12), $18.00 to $20.00

Reservations—Two months for dorm rooms, four to six months for standard rooms, nine months for cabins w/o fireplace, and one year for cabins with fireplace.

Comments—The rim cabins are a true experience, and those with fireplaces have the distinctive smell of pinyon pine when fires are going.

Phantom Ranch

Grand Canyon National Park Lodges
P.O. Box 699
South Rim
Grand Canyon, Arizona 86023
(602) 638-2401

Season—Year-round

Rates—Dormitory, $11.00
Cabins, $38.50, plus $7.00 per extra person
meals, breakfast-$6.25, lunch-$5.00, and dinner-$9.40
Overnight stay with mule ride in and out, including three meals, $137.00 per person

Reservations—Six to nine months ahead for either accommodations or accommodations and mule ride.

Comments—There are a number of park restrictions on hiking and camping in the canyon, and there are weight limits for the mule rides. Check all of these out thoroughly before leaving on a trip to Grand Canyon.

Grand Canyon Lodge

TWA Services, Inc.
North Rim
Grand Canyon, Arizona 86023
(801) 586-7686

Season—Mid-May to mid-October

Rates—Regular cabins, $36.05
Deluxe cabins with private porch, $45.32

Reservations—Three to four months in advance.

Comments—The Grand Canyon Lodge offers a very different view of the Grand Canyon, and is well worth the extra effort to reach.

GREAT SMOKY MOUNTAINS NATIONAL PARK

Wonderland Club Hotel

Route 2
Gatlinburg, Tennessee 37738
(615) 436-5490

Season—Memorial Day Weekend to October 31
Rates—Rooms w/o bath (6), $32.00
Rooms with bath (17), $45.00
2 bedrooms with bath (4), $60.00
Reservations—Four to six weeks for June, July, and August. One week for September, and six months for October.
Comments—October is the time the forest's colors are the most beautiful, and the Wonderland Club Hotel is surrounded by red and yellow woods then.

Le Conte Lodge
Le Conte Lodge, Inc.
P.O. Box 350
Gatlinburg, Tennessee 37738
(615) 436-4473
Season—First of April to end of October
Rates—Rooms (with dinner and breakfast)
adult—$27.00
child (under 10)—$18.00
Reservations—Reservations for summer weekends and for October need to be made by first of the year. Summer weekdays are usually reserved by 1st of April.
Comments—Guests who bring their own sleeping bags get a $1.50 a night discount, and guests who stay two or more nights get lunch.

MT. RAINIER NATIONAL PARK
National Park Inn
Mt. Rainier Hospitality Service
Star Route
Ashford, Washington 98304
(206) 475-6260 from October 1 to mid-May
(206) 569-2706 from mid-May to October 1.
Season—Weekends and holidays from January 1 to March 31.
Every day from April 1 to December 31.
Rates—Rooms w/o bath, $21.75
Rooms with bath, $35.50
Suites, $47.50
Extra person $5.00
Reservations—One to two months in advance.

Paradise Inn
Mt. Rainier Hospitality Service
Star Route
Ashford, Washington 98304
(206) 475-6260 from October 1 to mid-May
(206) 569-2706 from mid-May to October 1

Season—June 1 to October 1

Rates—Rooms w/o bath, $23.75
Rooms with bath $40.50
Suite, $54.00

Reservations—Four to six months in advance.

Comments—The alpine flowers bloom in profusion in late August and early September, depending on how late the snowpack stays.

OLYMPIC NATIONAL PARK

Lake Crescent Lodge
National Park Concessions, Inc.
Star Route 1, Box 11
Port Angeles, Washington 98362
(206) 928-3211

Season—Mid-May to end of October. Possibility of opening year-round in several years

Rates—Lodge rooms (5), $22.50 plus $4.50 per extra person
Cottages 1-room (17), $26.00 plus $4.50 per extra person
Cottages 2-room (8), $31.50 plus $4.50 per extra person
Fireplace cottages (4), $43.50 plus $4.50 per extra person
Motel rooms (20), $43.50 plus $4.50 per extra person

Reservations—Two to four months for cottages and motel rooms. Can often find lodge rooms available on drop-in basis.

Comments—Although the lodge rooms are the last to rent they offer a warm, comfortable place with a great view of Lake Crescent. Remember that you share a bath down the hall.

OREGON CAVES NATIONAL MONUMENT

Oregon Caves Chateau

Season—Mid-June to mid-September

Rates—Lodge, $33.00 to $44.00
Cottages, $32.00 to $36.00

Reservations—There are almost always vacancies at the Chateau.

Comments—Well worth the trip if you just want a quiet lodge to relax and rest.

YELLOWSTONE NATIONAL PARK

Lake Hotel

TWA Services, Inc.
Yellowstone National Park, Wyoming 82190
(307) 344-7311

Season—Mid-May to end of September
Rates—$23.00 to $47.00
Reservations—one to two months in advance.

Old Faithful Inn

TWA Services, Inc.
Yellowstone National Park, Wyoming 82190
(307) 344-7311

Season—Mid-May to mid-October
Rates—$23.00 to $47.00
Reservations—four to six months in advance.
Comments—There are five rooms at the Inn that overlook the Upper Geyser Basin and which were used as Presidential suites in the early years of the Inn. These are w/o bath and are $23.00 rooms, but try to get one of them if you can.

Roosevelt Lodge

TWA Services, Inc.
Yellowstone National Park, Wyoming 82190
(307) 344-7311

Season—Mid-June to early September
Rates—Rustic shelters (12), $11.00
wood stove, no linens or running water
Roughrider cabins (50), $12.00
wood heat, no running water, but linens
Family cabins (9), $23.00
cabins with half bath
Standard cabins (7), $35.00
cabins with full bath
Reservations—Two weeks to a month in advance.
Comments—Most guests stay for at least a week at Roosevelt.

Mammoth Hot Springs Hotel and Cabins

TWA Services, Inc.
Yellowstone National Park, Wyoming 82190
(307) 344-7311

Season—Late-May to mid-September. Also open some in winter
Rates—Rooms w/o bath (69), $23.00
Rooms with bath (88), $36.00
Deluxe rooms (26), $47.00
Cabins (111), $18.00 to $35.00
Reservations—Two weeks to a month in advance, although has vacancies occasionally.
Comment—Most guests use Mammoth Hot Springs as a stopover, but there are a number of things to do in the area that could take up to a week.

YOSEMITE NATIONAL PARK

Wawona Hotel
Yosemite Park and Curry Company
Yosemite National Park, California 95389
(209) 372-1445
Season—May 1 to November 1
Rates—Rooms w/o bath, $36.00
Rooms with bath, $51.00
Reservations—Six months in advance.

The Ahwahnee
Yosemite Park and Curry Company
Yosemite National Park, California 95389
(209) 372-1445
Season—Year-round
Rates—Double occupancy rooms, $117.00
Penthose, $157.00
Private sitting rooms adjacent to rooms, $109.00
Some mid-week ski packages are offered in winter, but rates vary.
Reservations—Six months to a year in advance. Only long-time guests can make reservations for the Bracebridge Dinner. All others have to apply, have their names put in a hat, and 1,000 are drawn. Application must be made at least a year ahead of time. Check with The Ahwahnee for current status of applications.
Comment—The Bracebridge Dinner is worth the effort, but if you can't make that, The Ahwahnee itself is just as rewarding. This is my favorite lodge in all the parks.

All rates quoted are from the 1982 season, and they are subject to change. These were used for comparative purposes only.